IS
SI:NG

Printed in the United States of America

First Printing, 2020

ISBN: 978-1-7347545-6-8

Press Here
410 S Michigan Ave Suite 420
Chicago, IL 60605

www.mattbodett.com

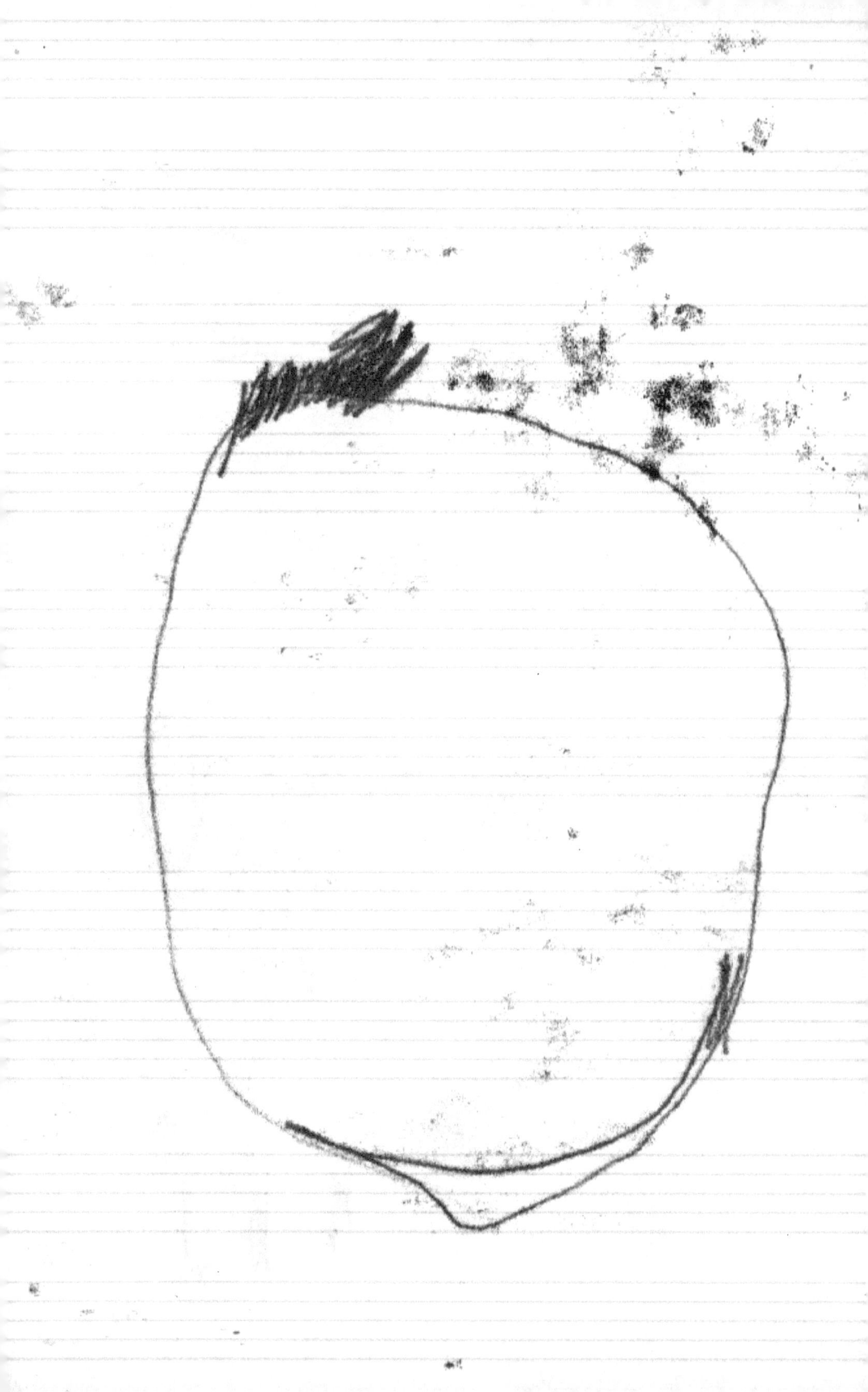

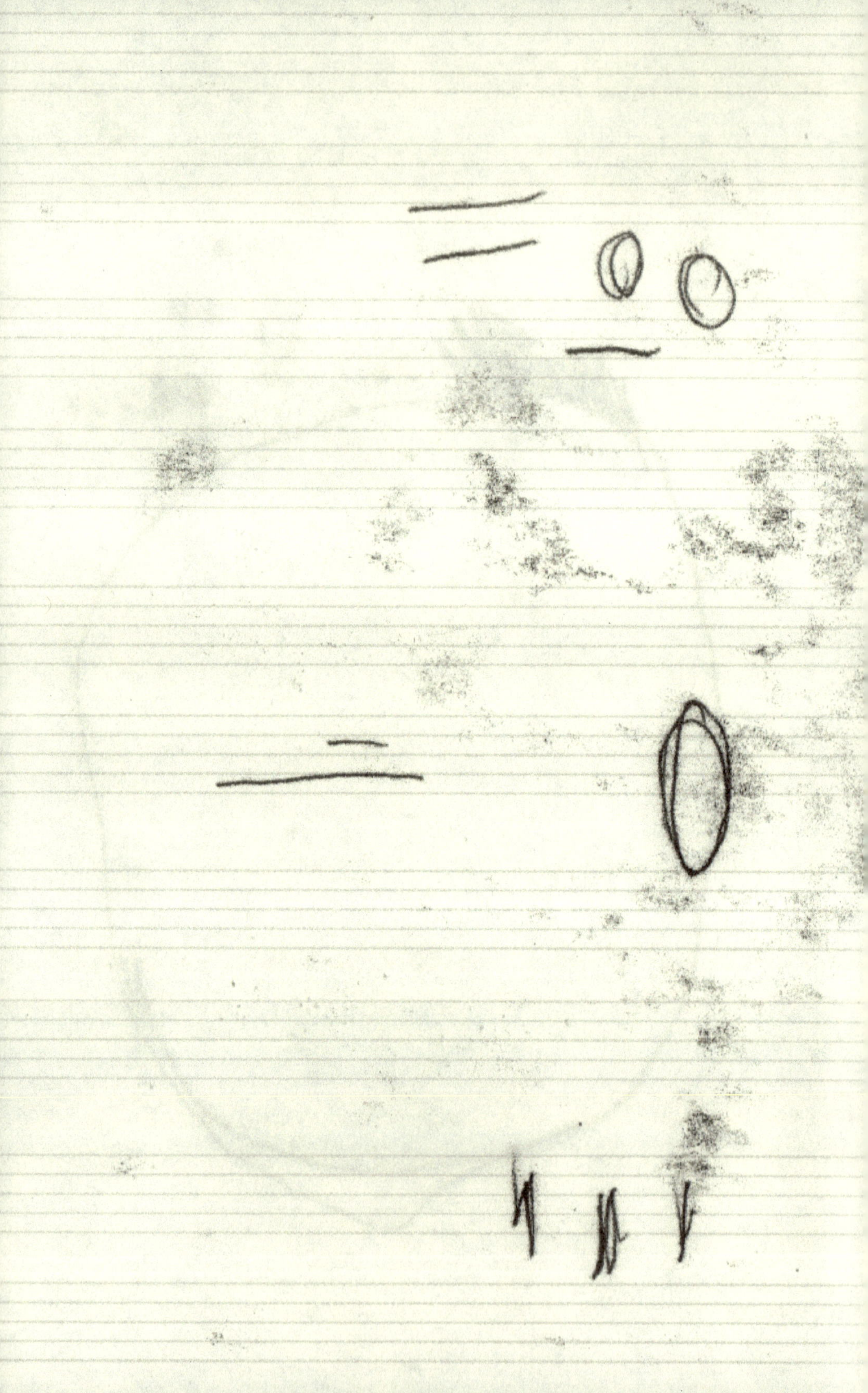

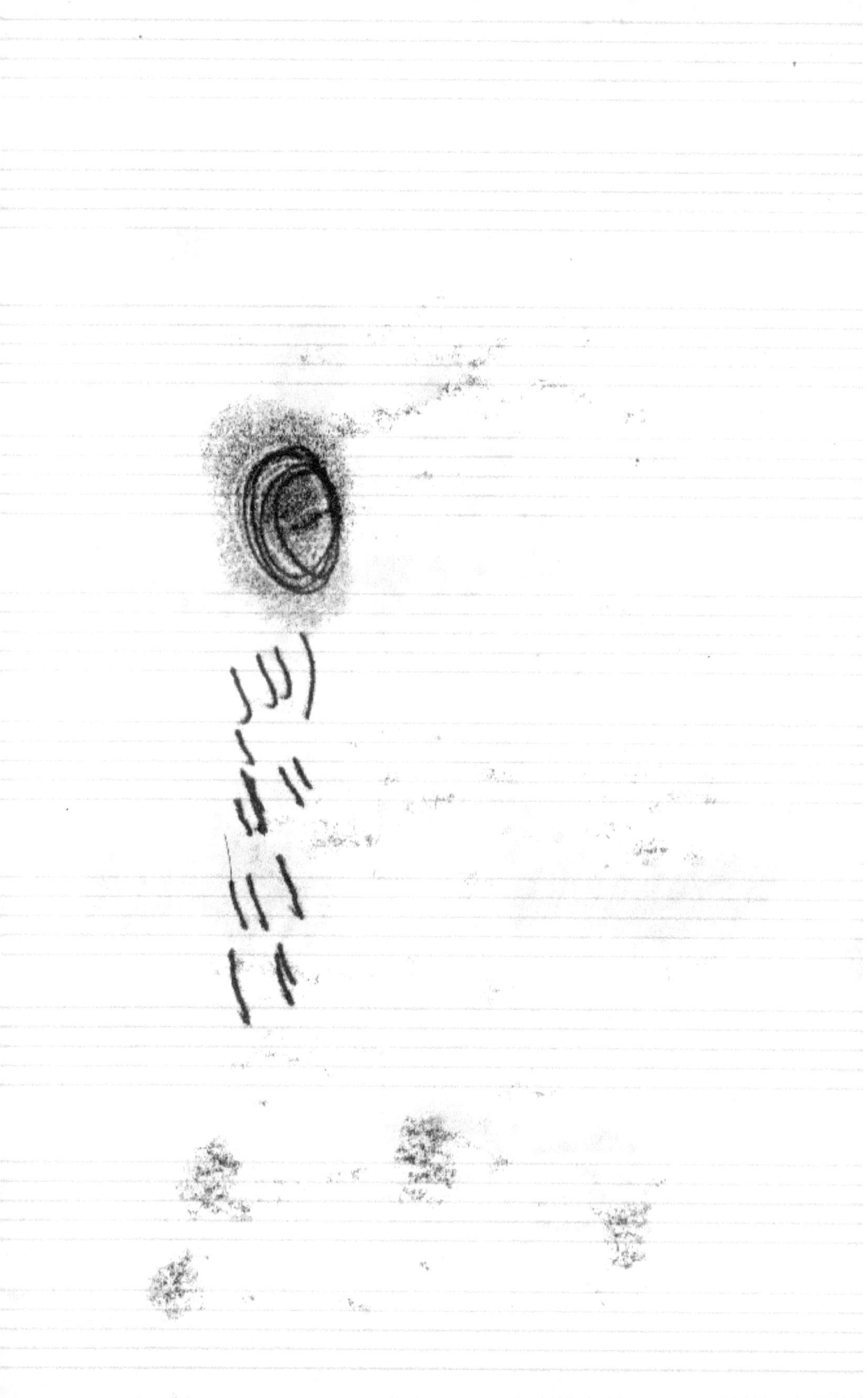

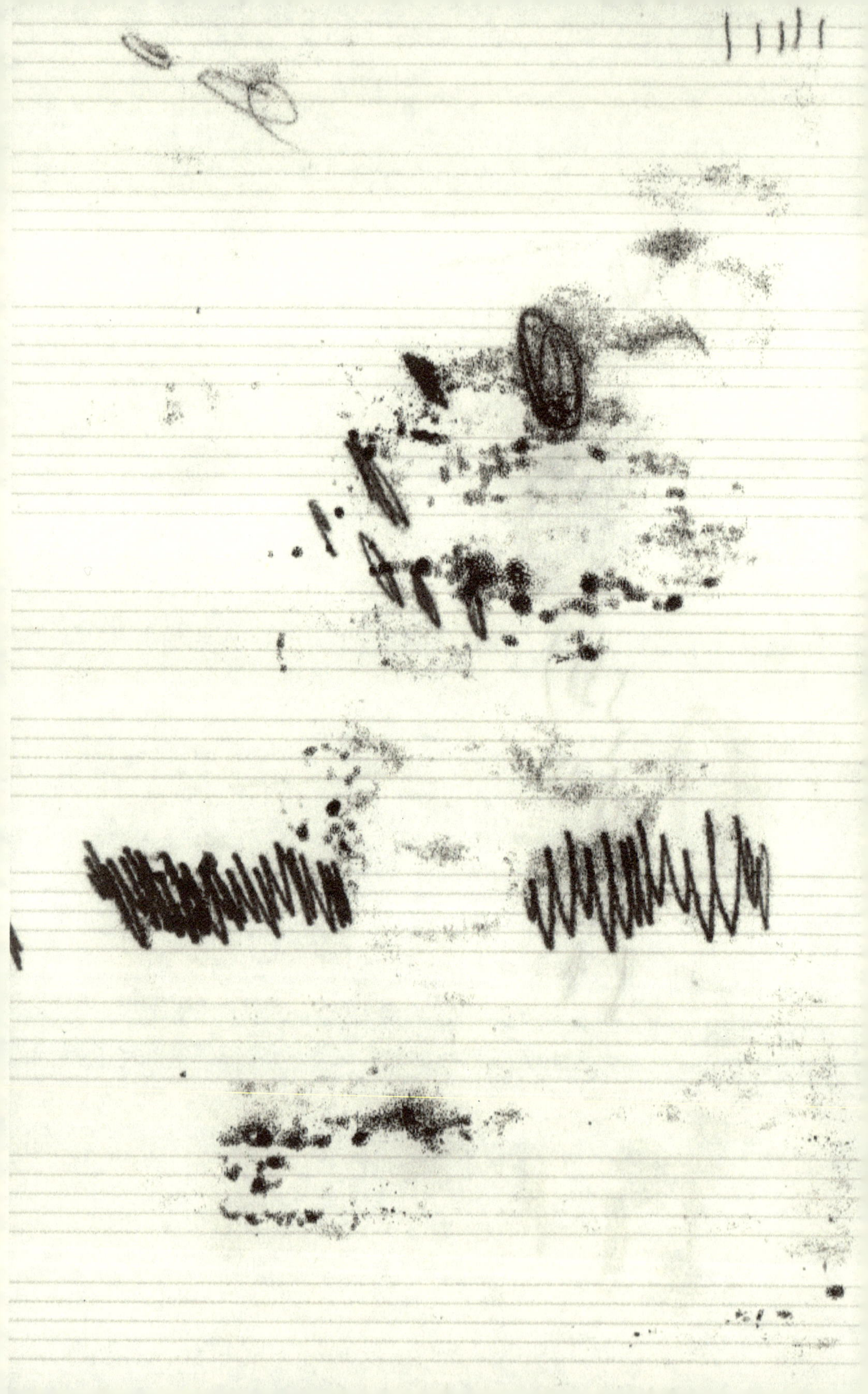

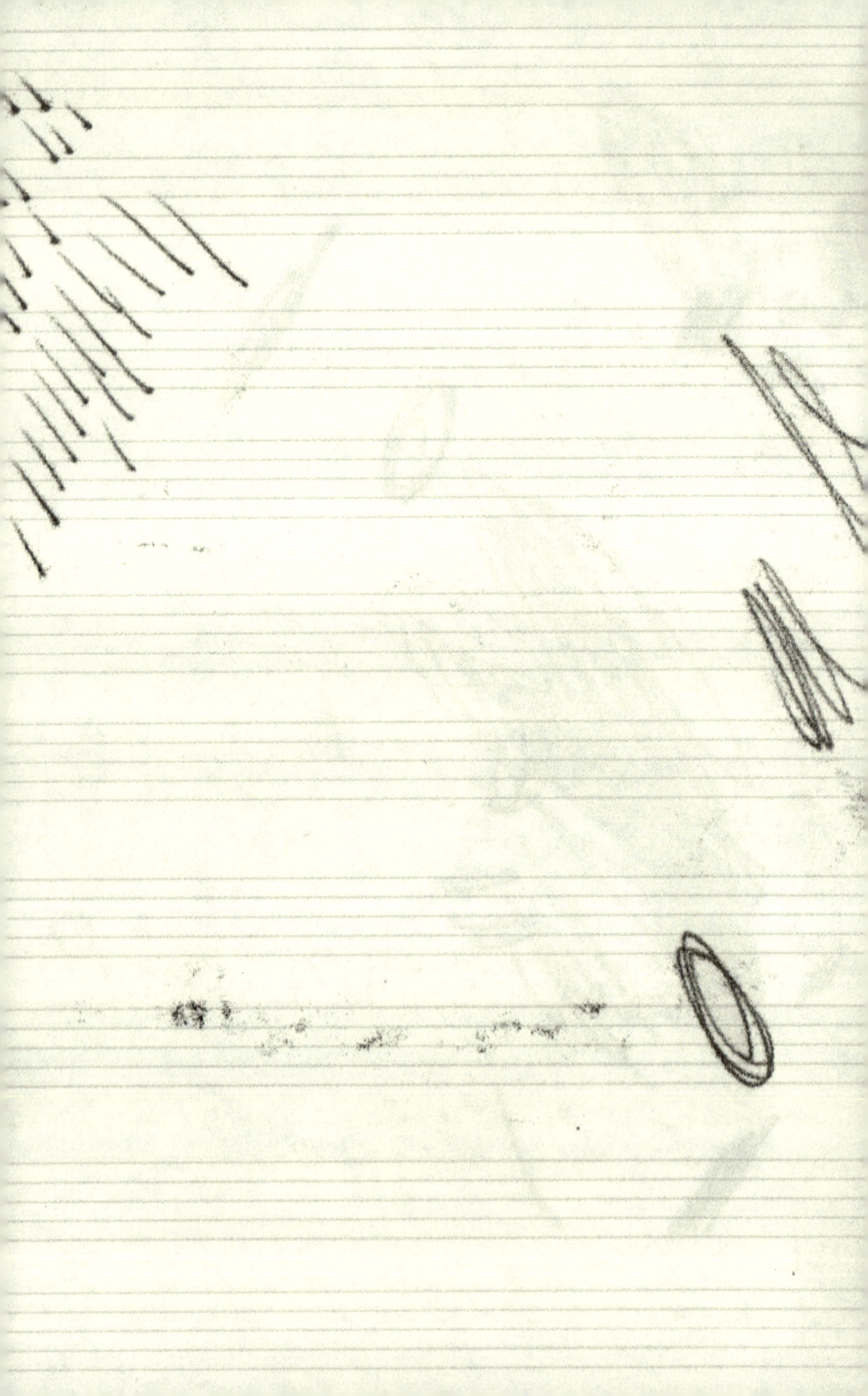

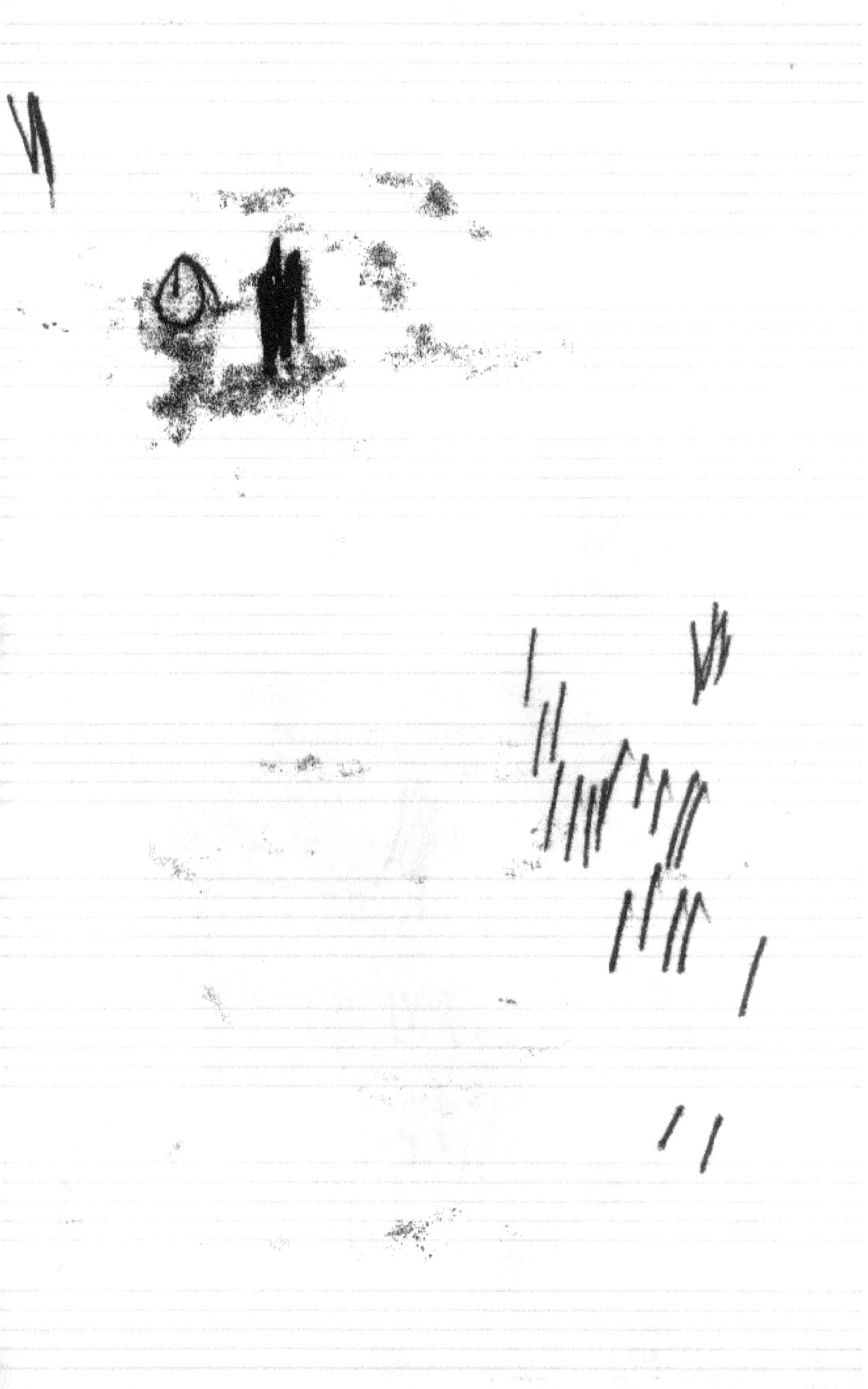

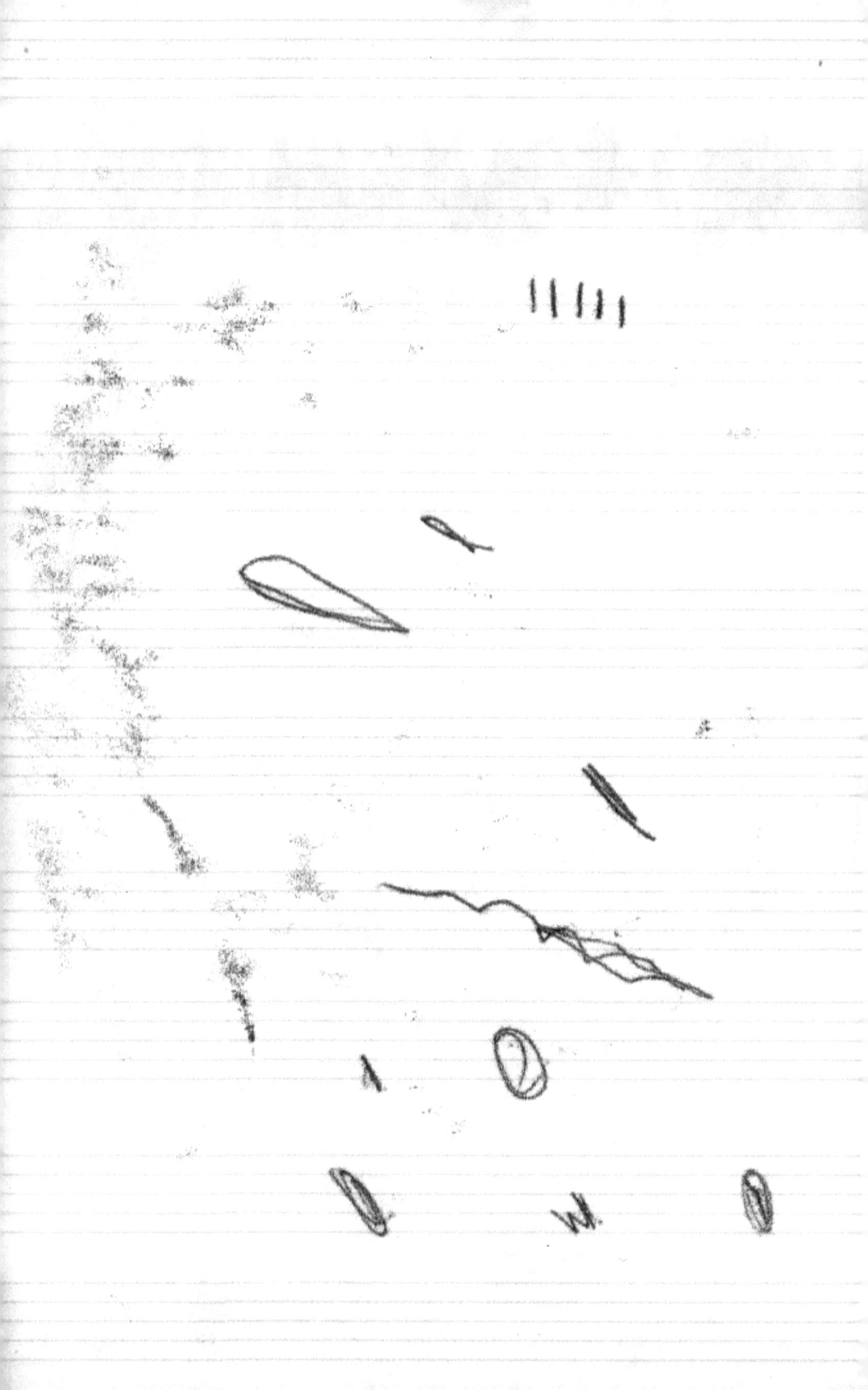

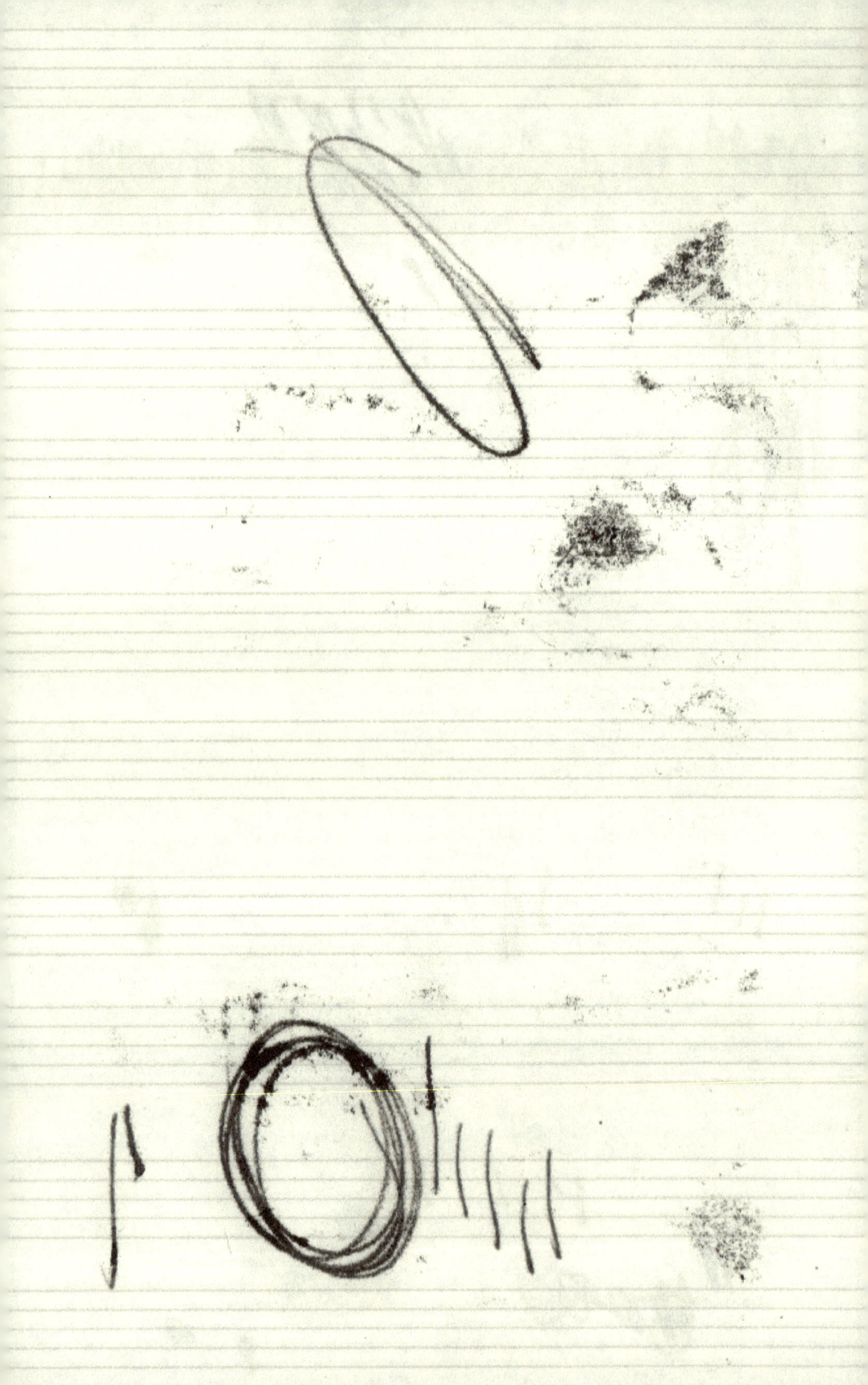

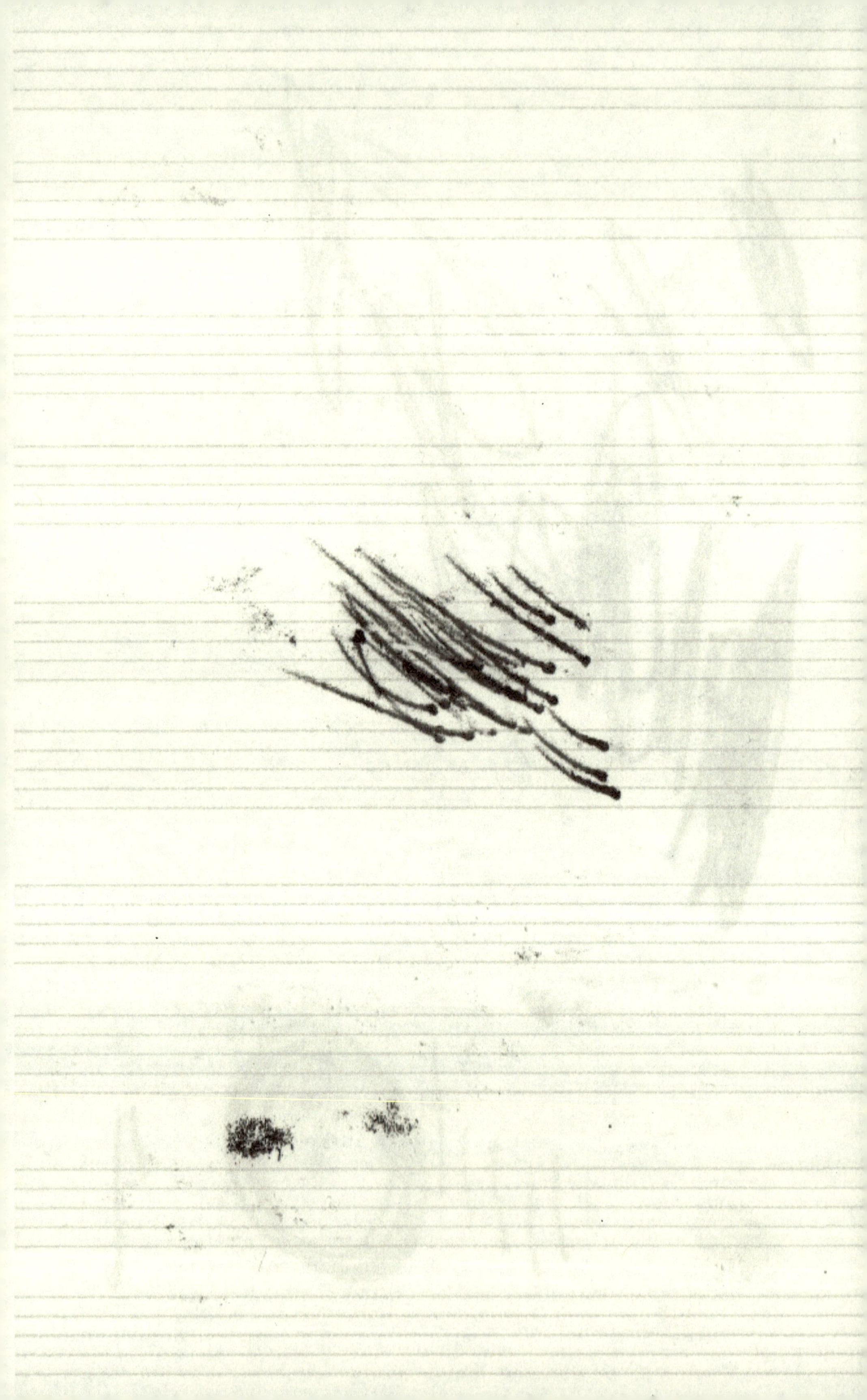

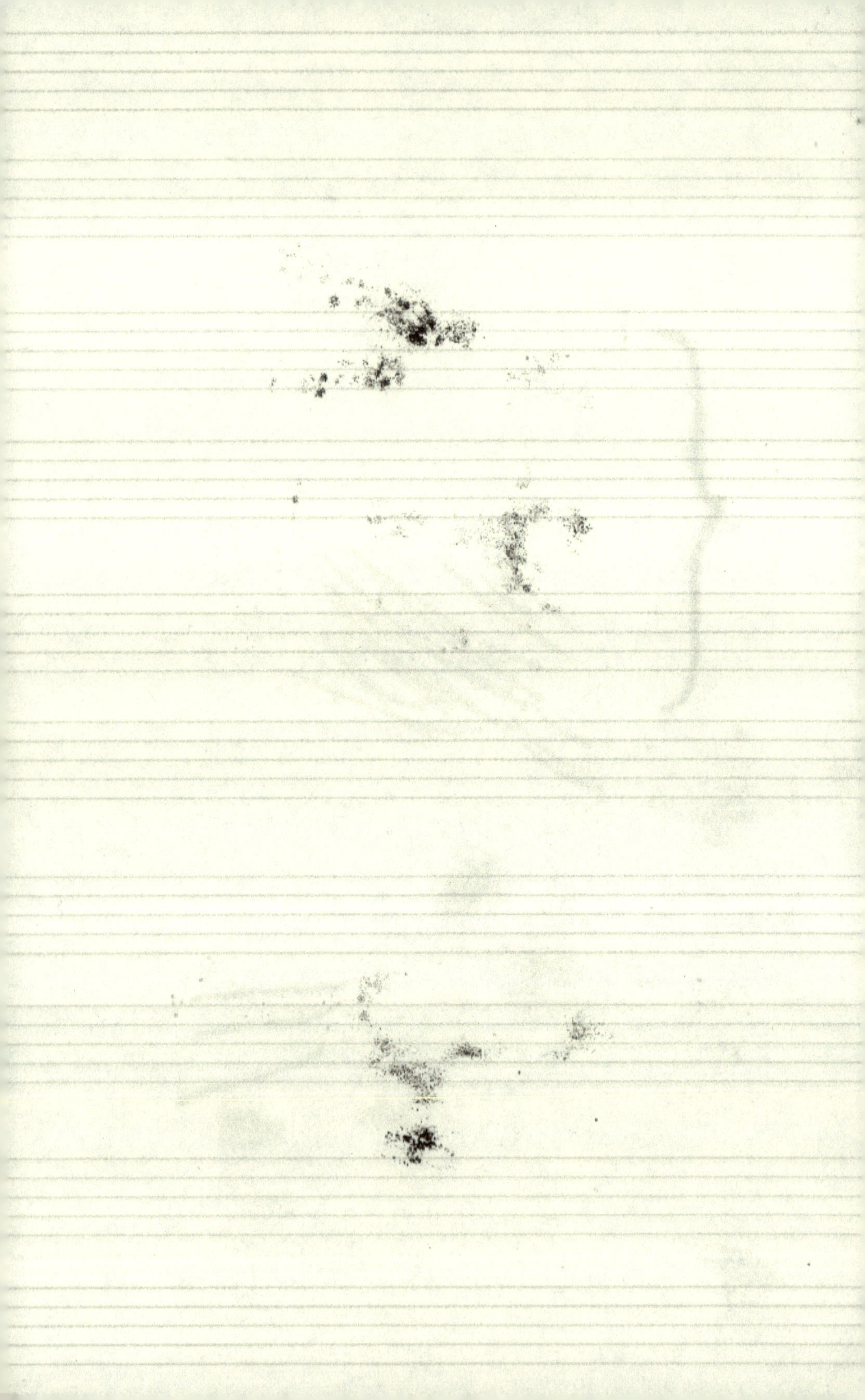

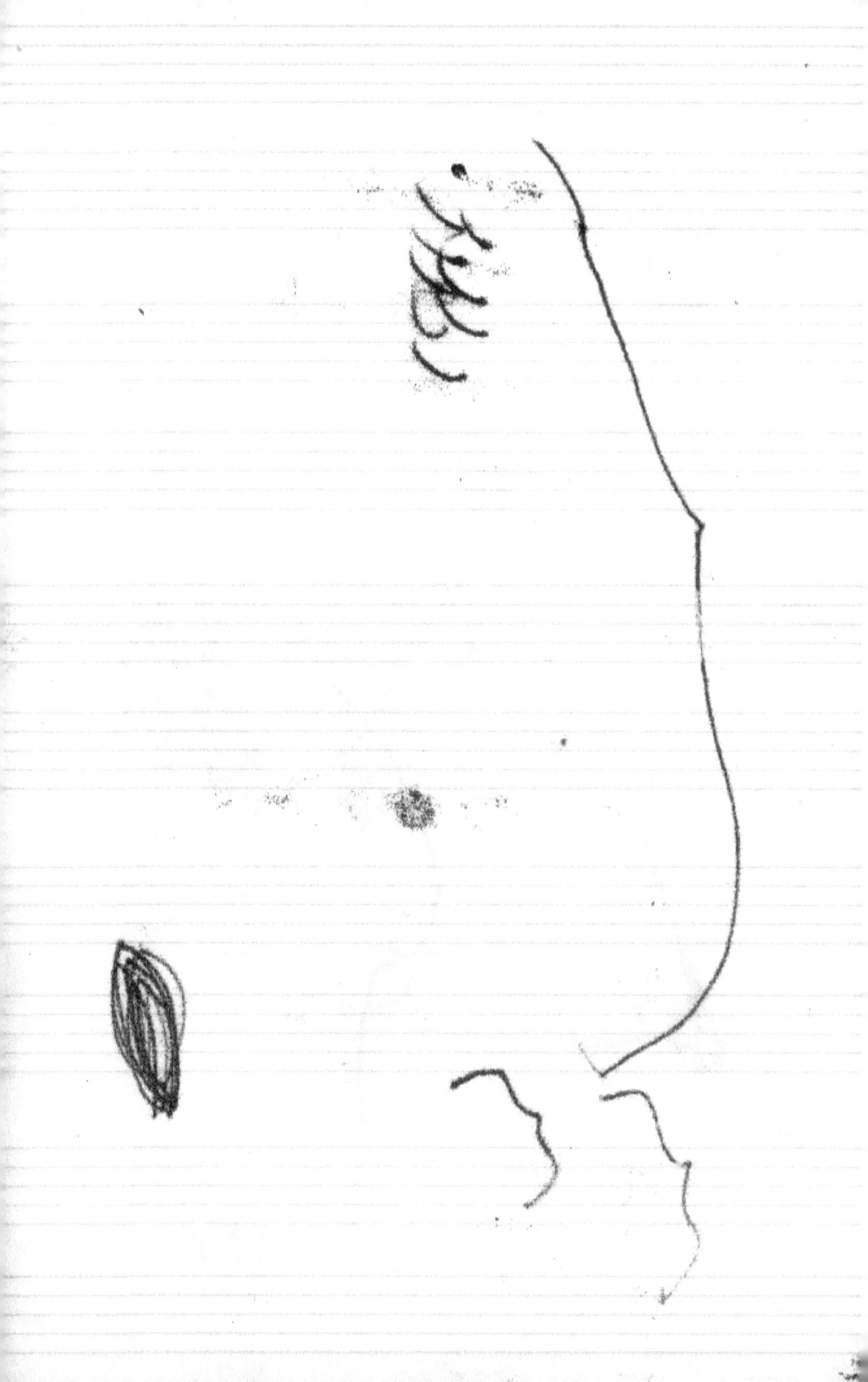

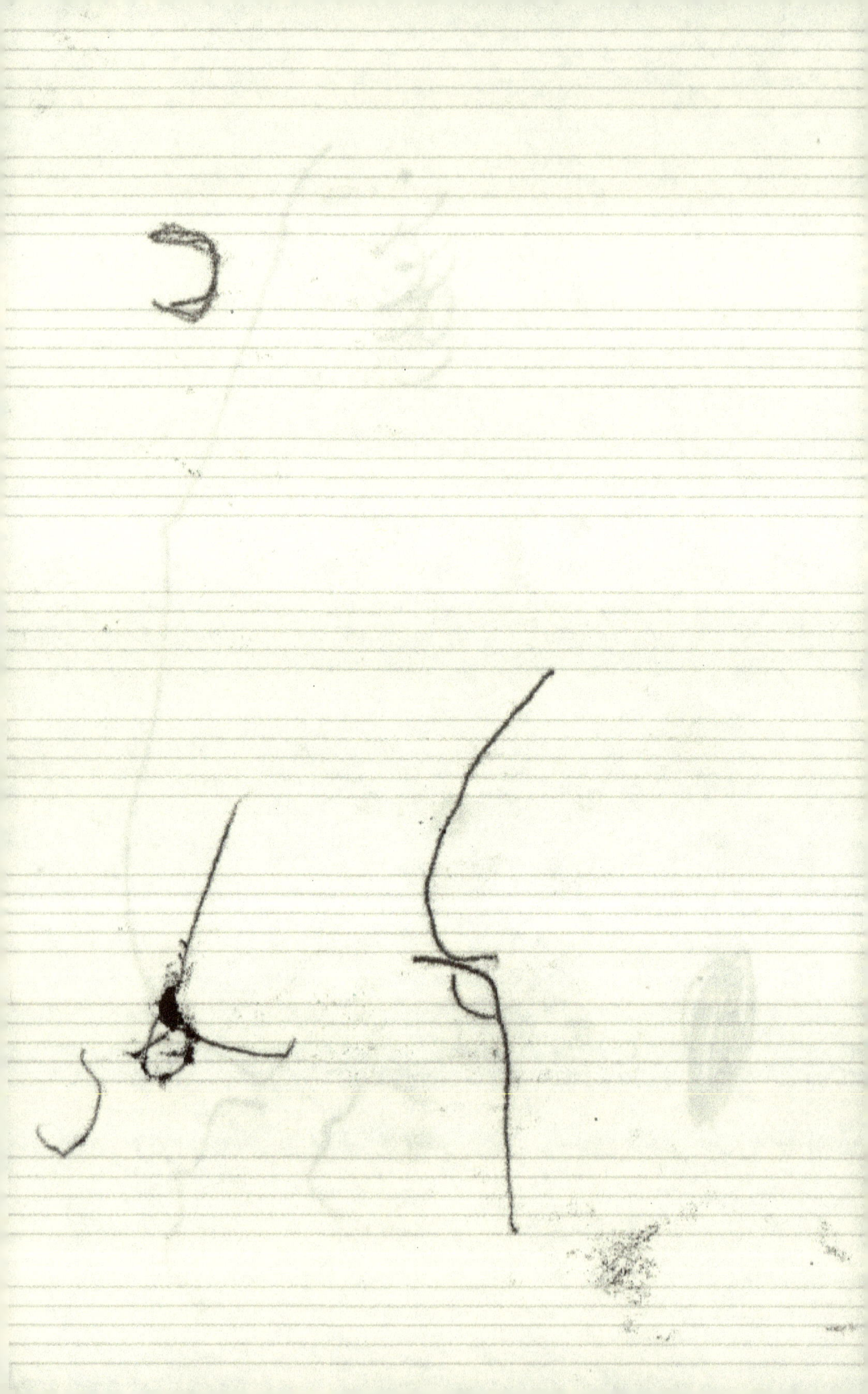

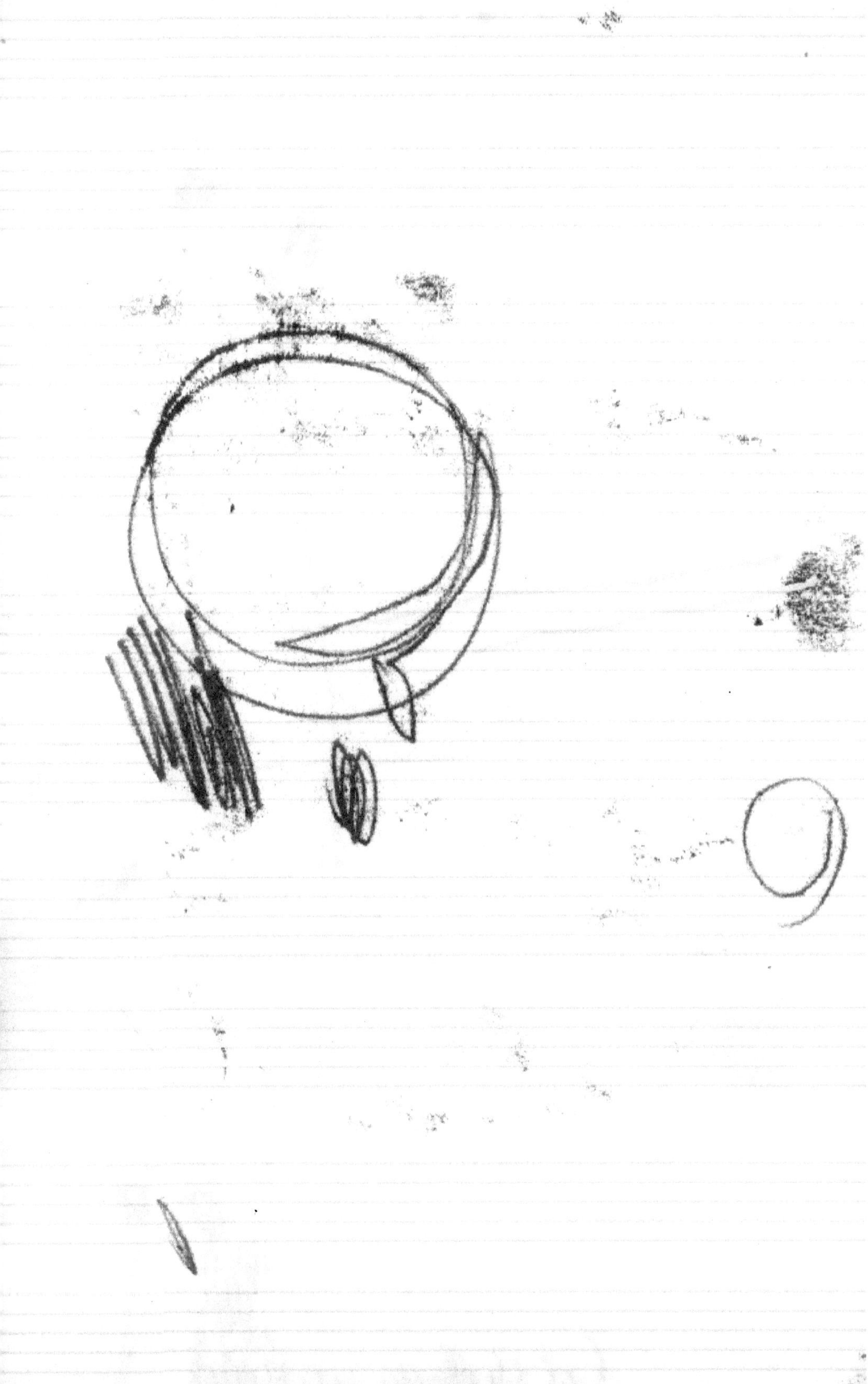

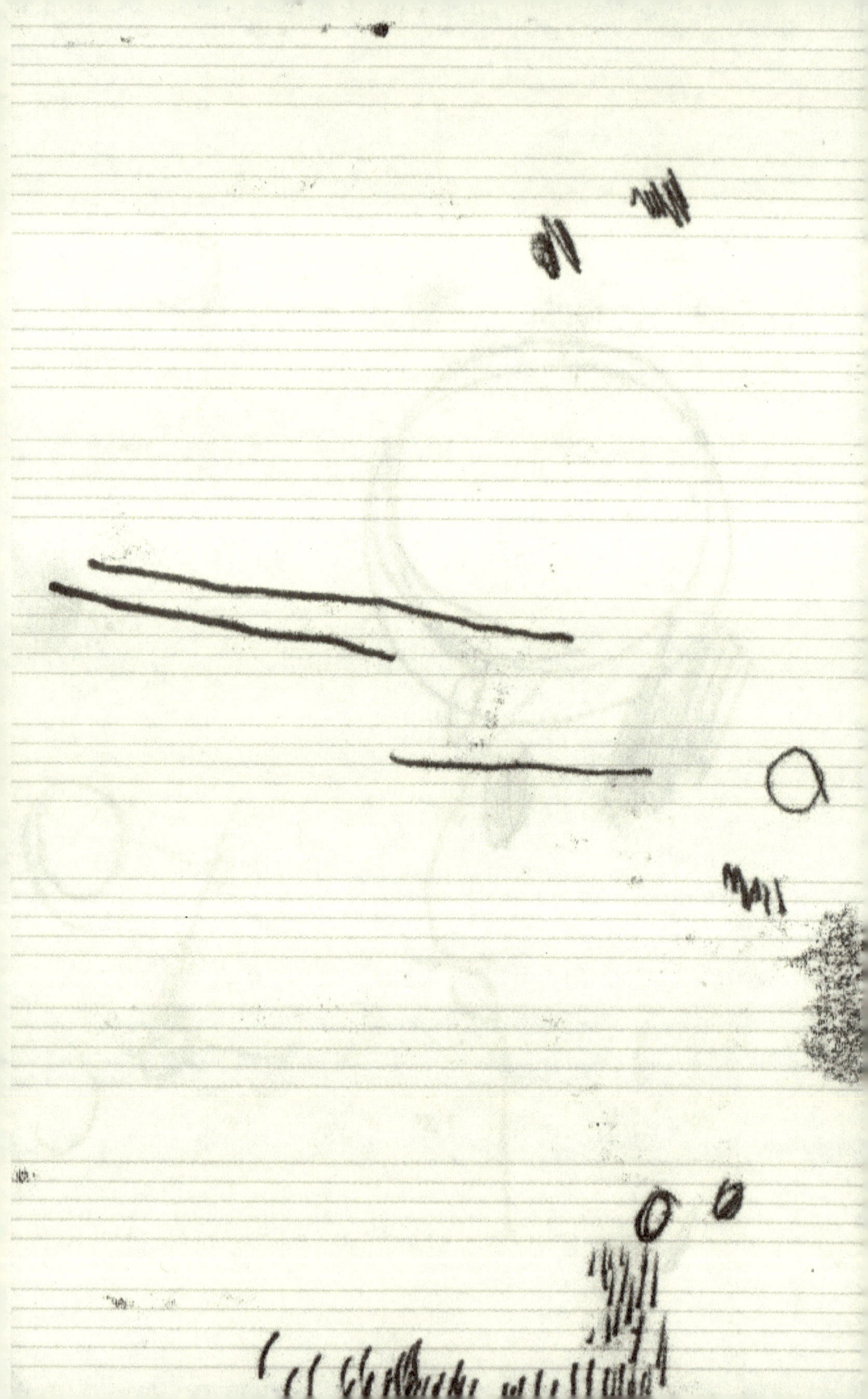

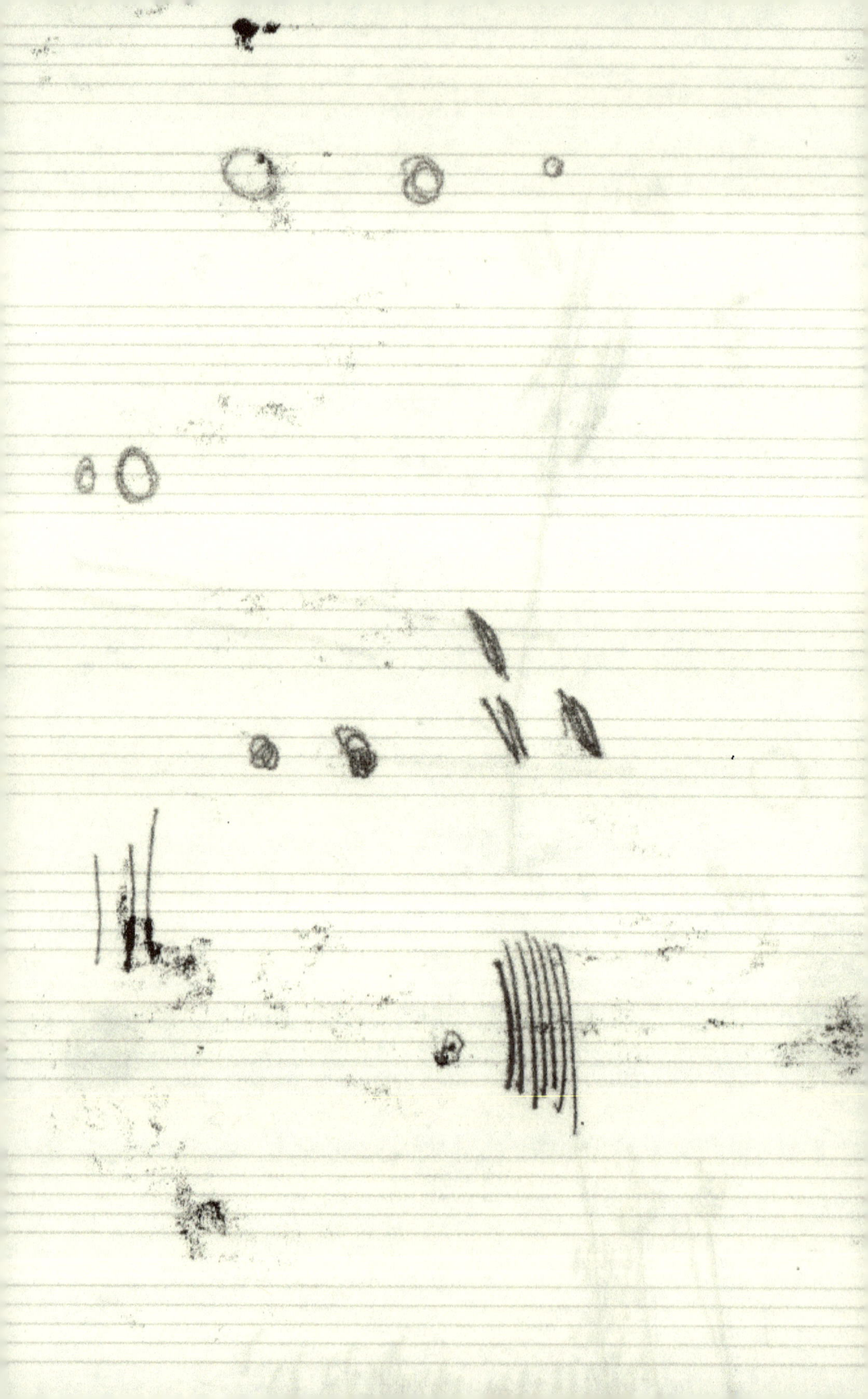

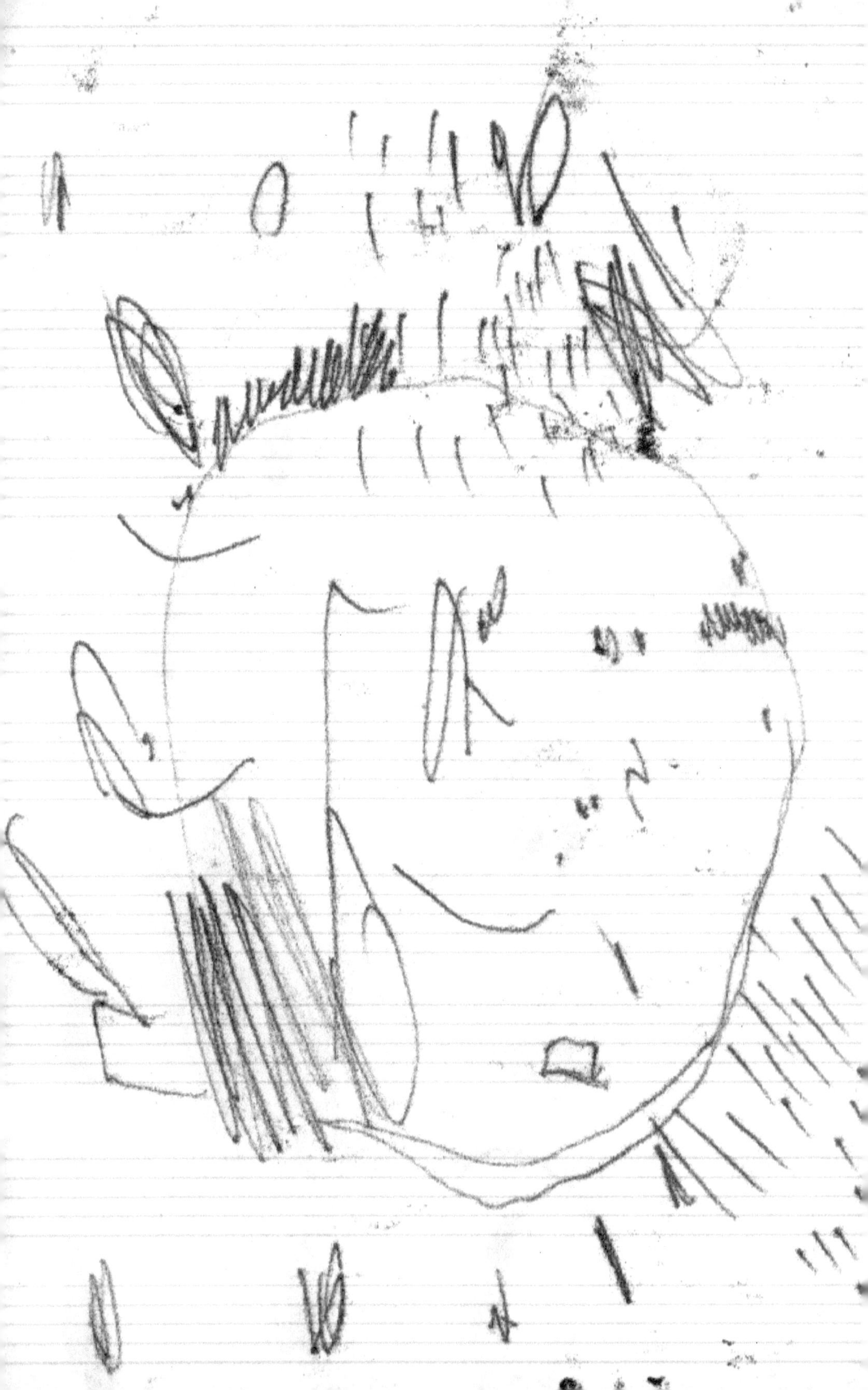

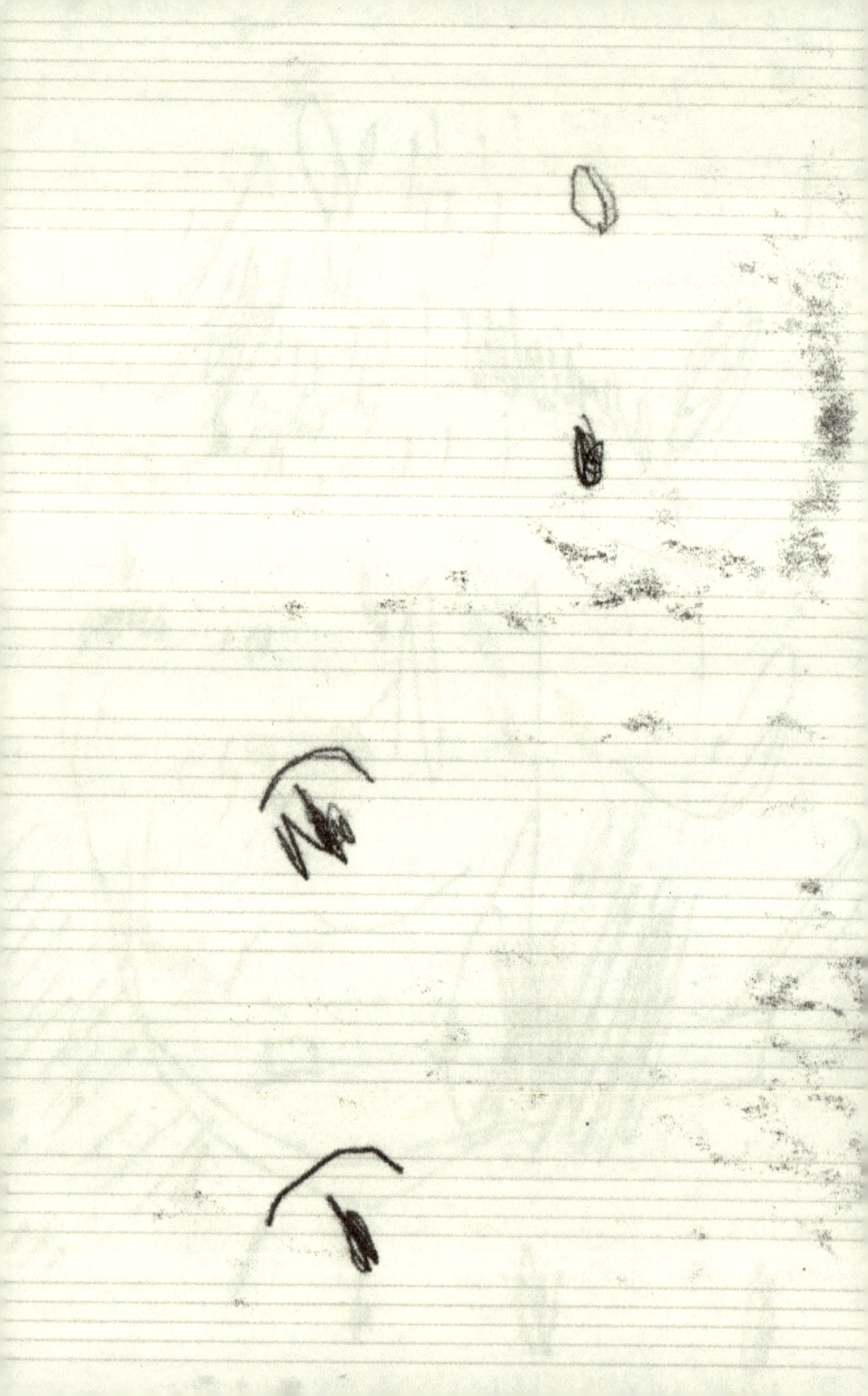

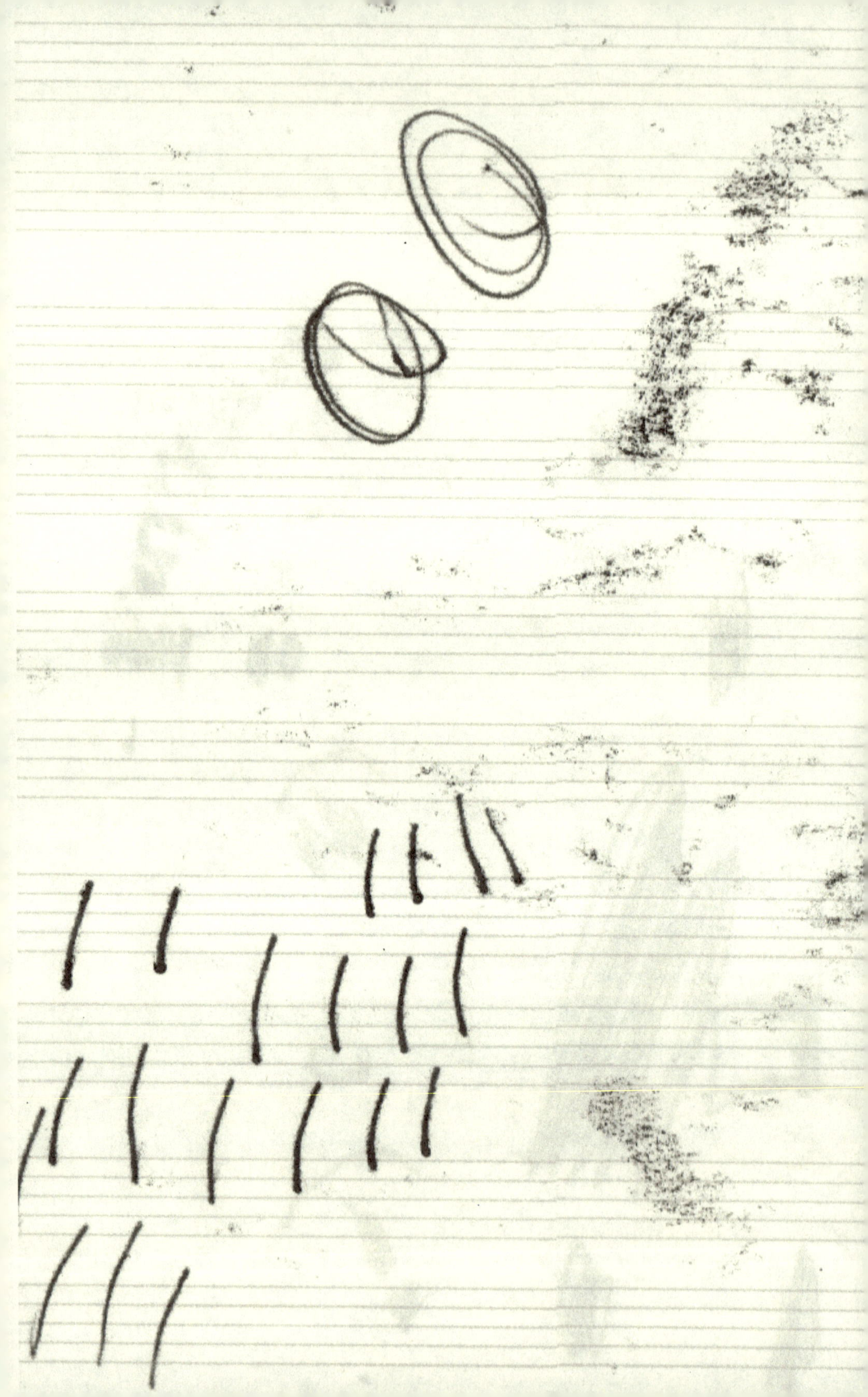

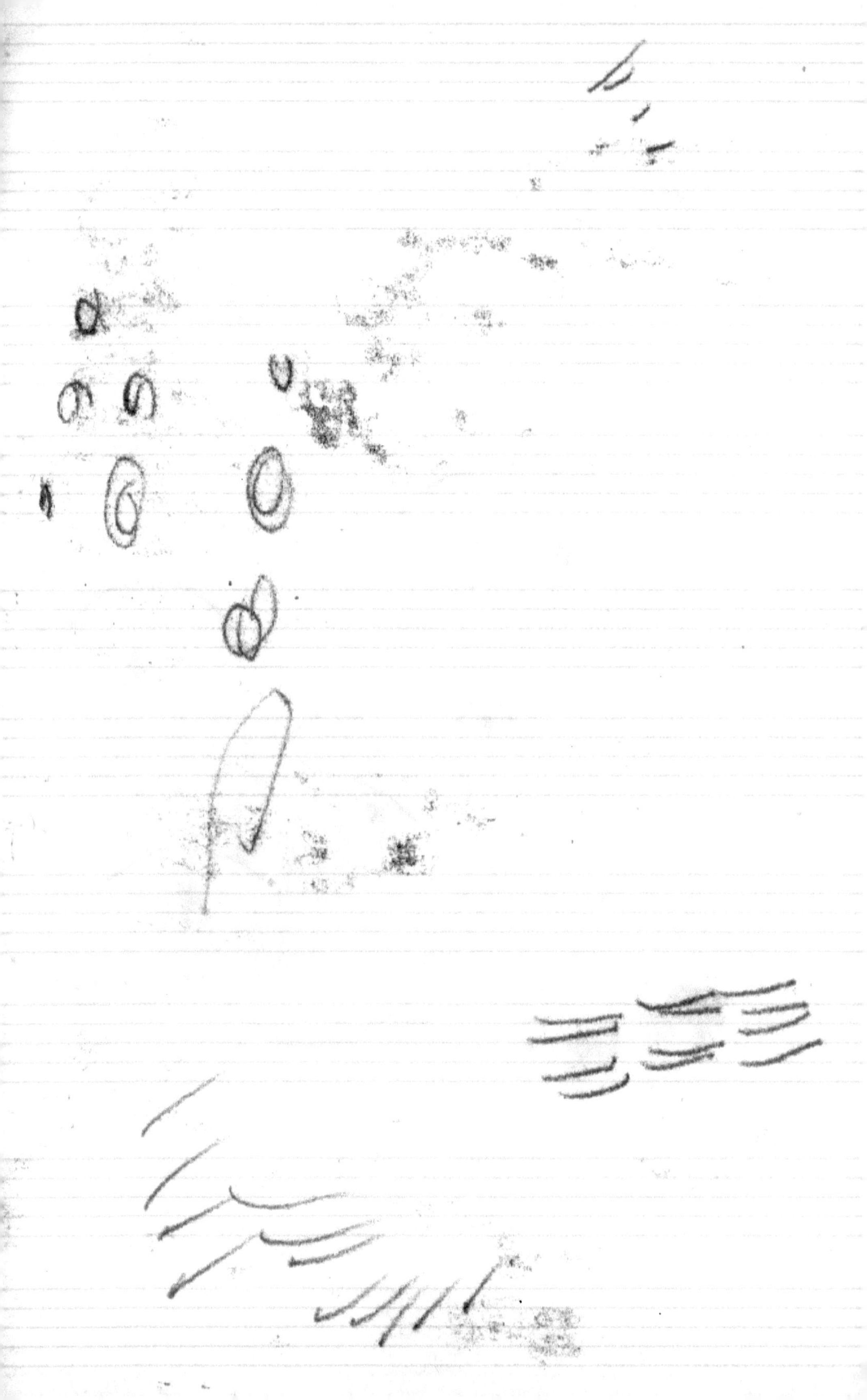

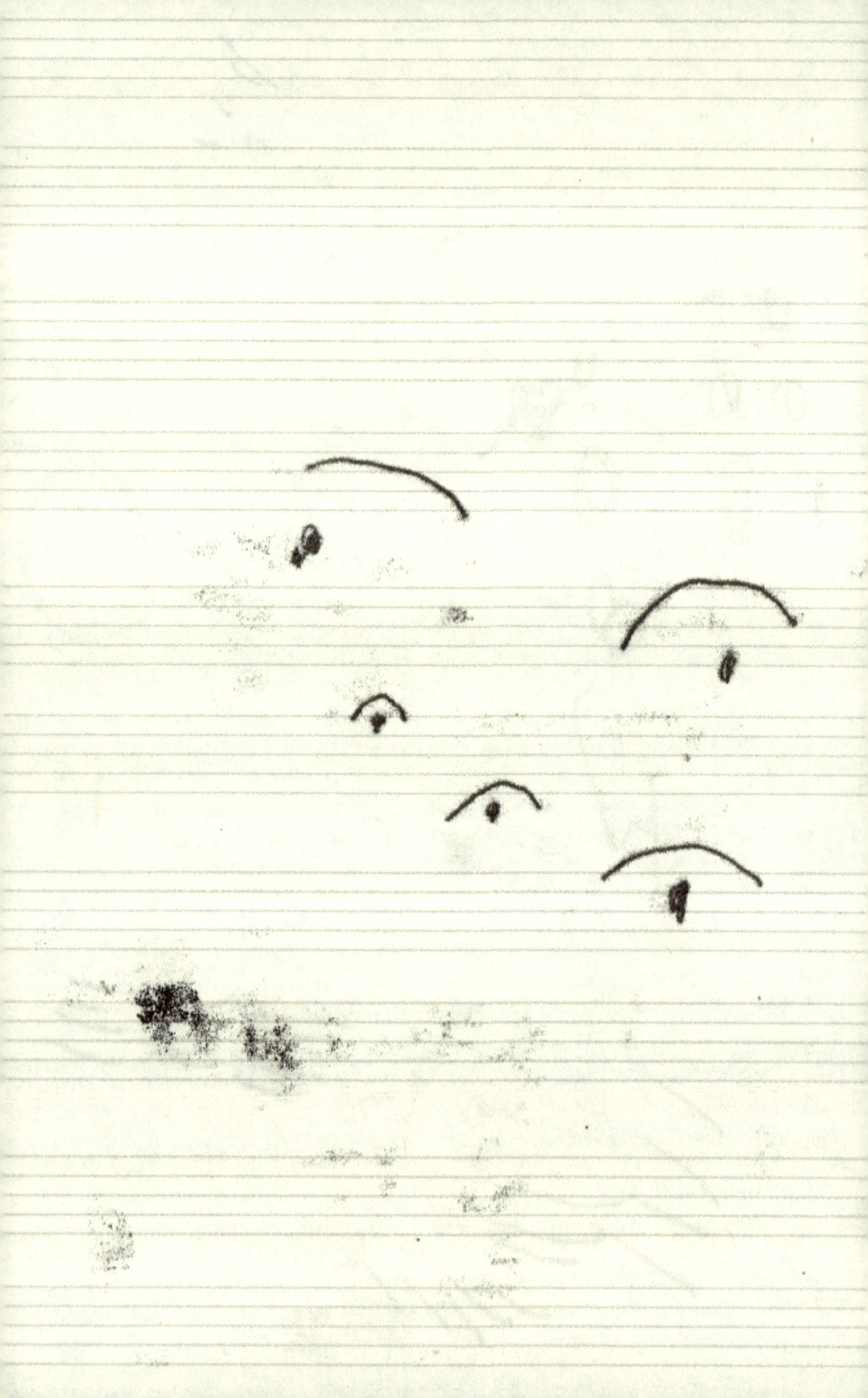

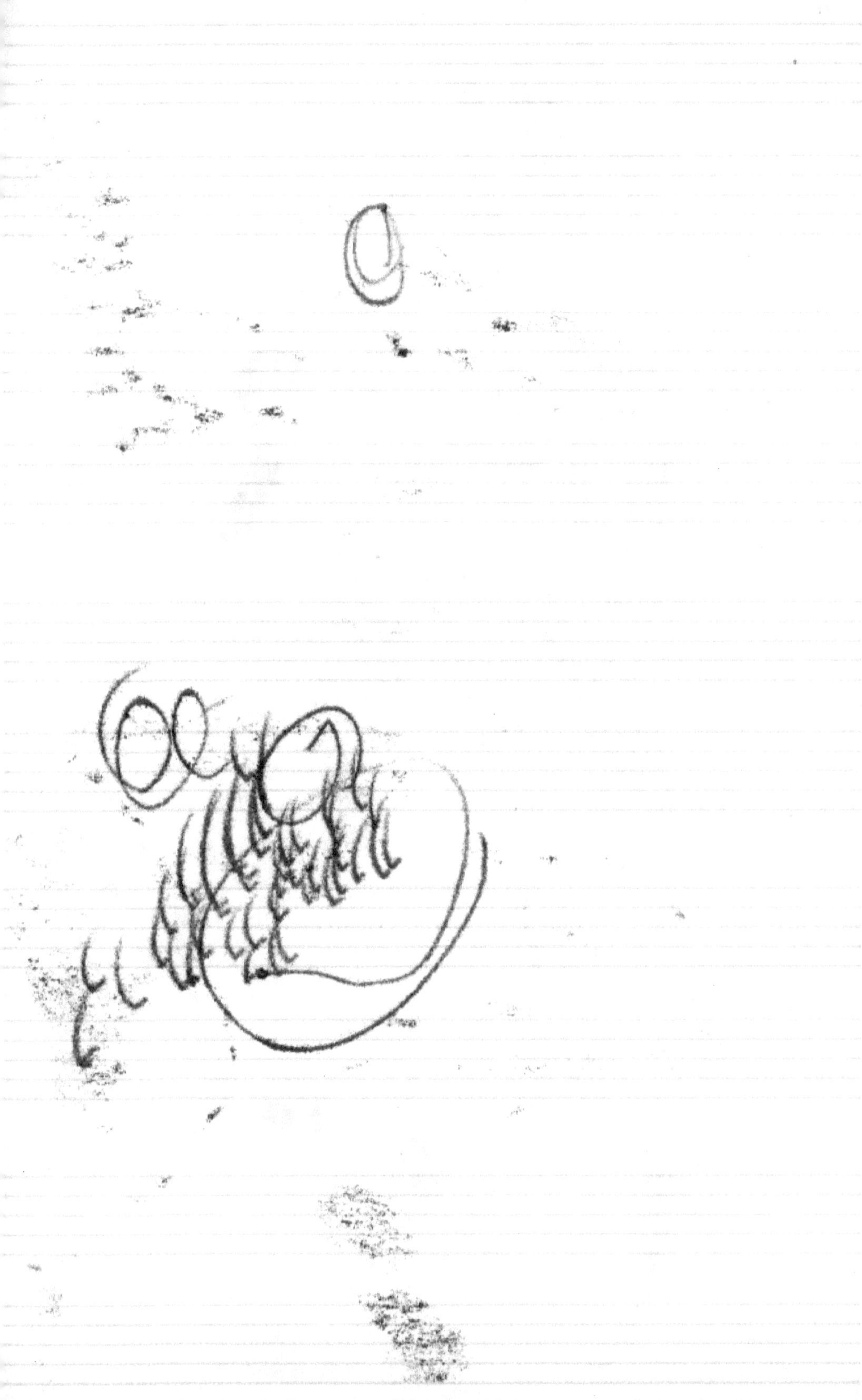

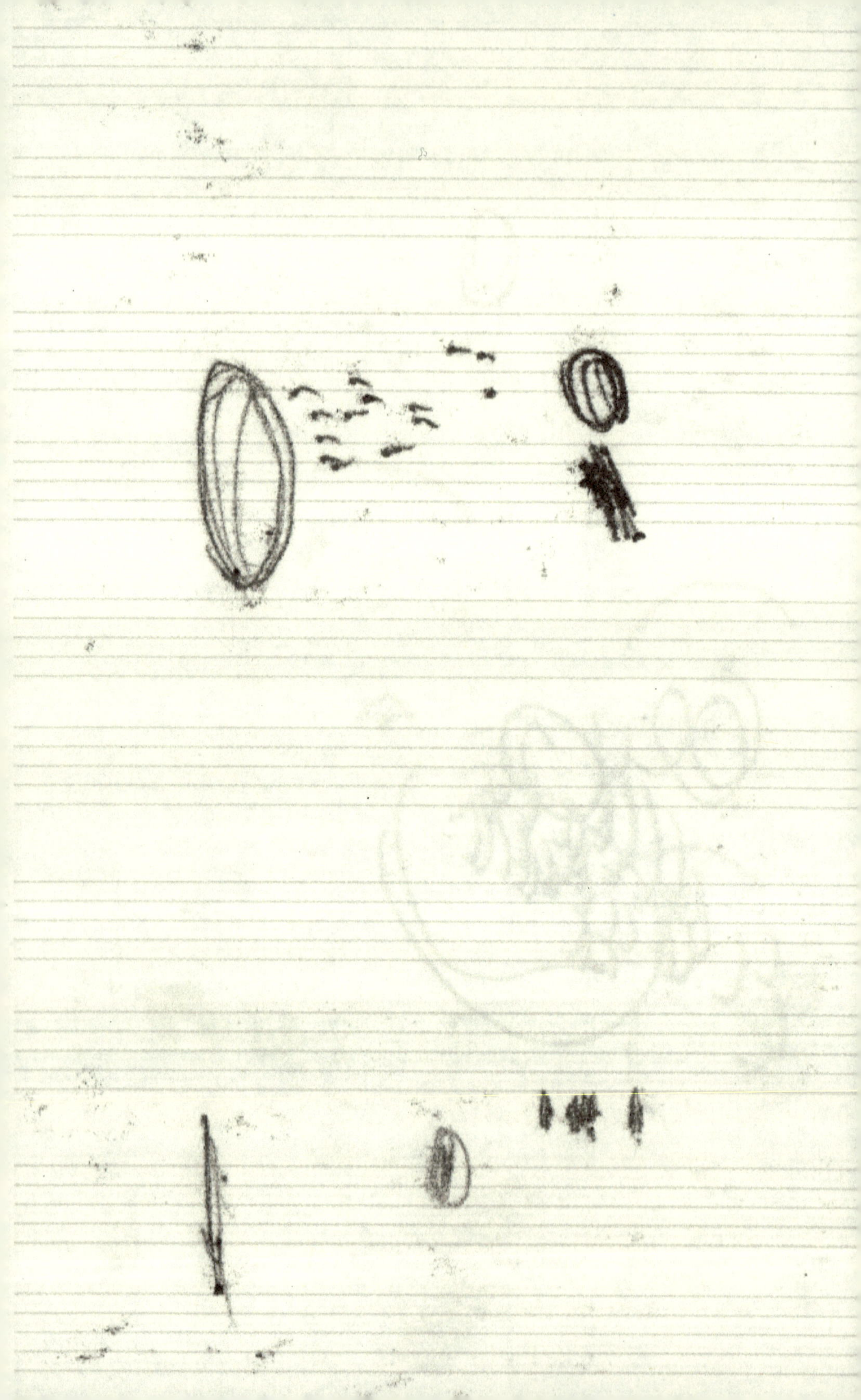

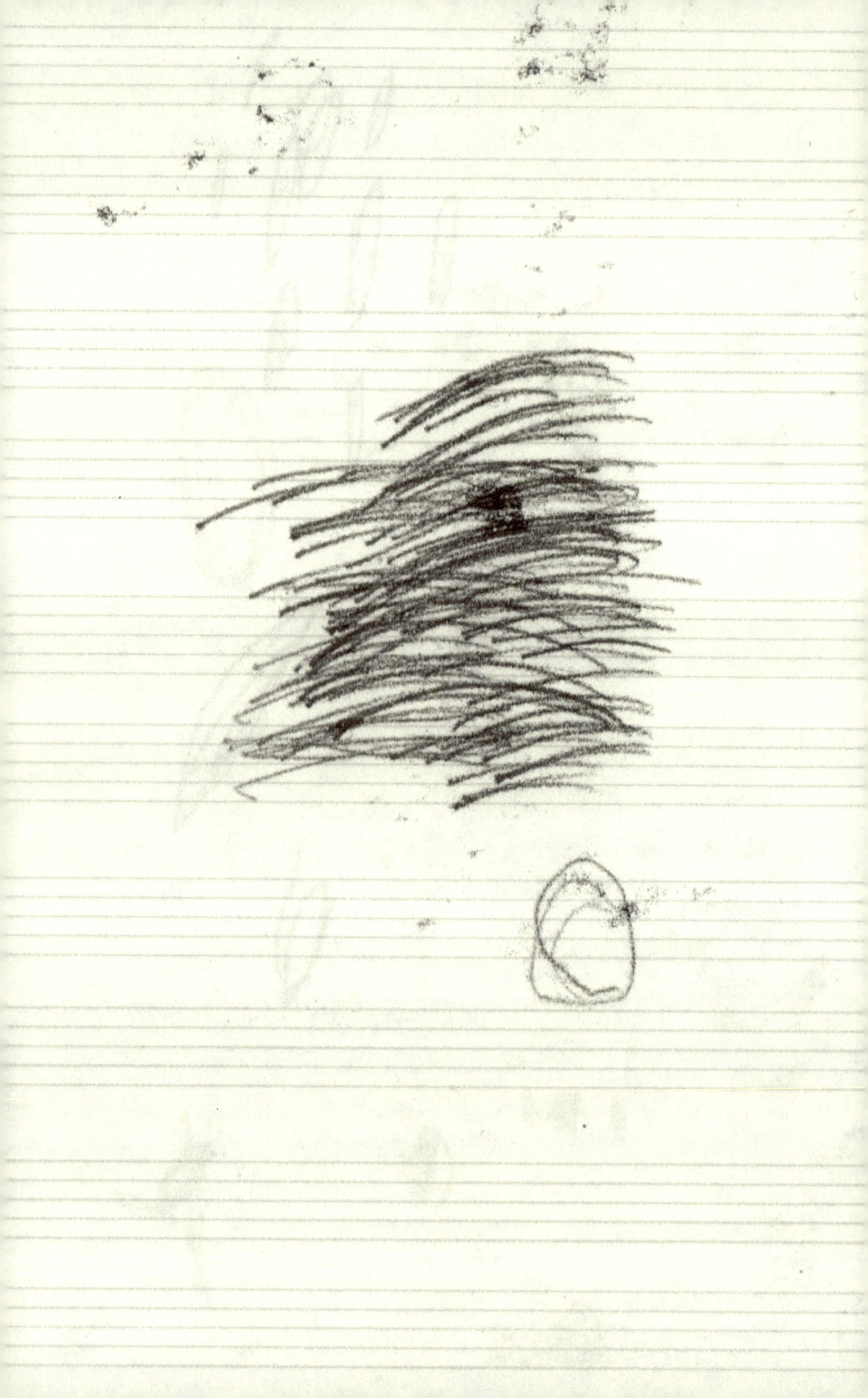

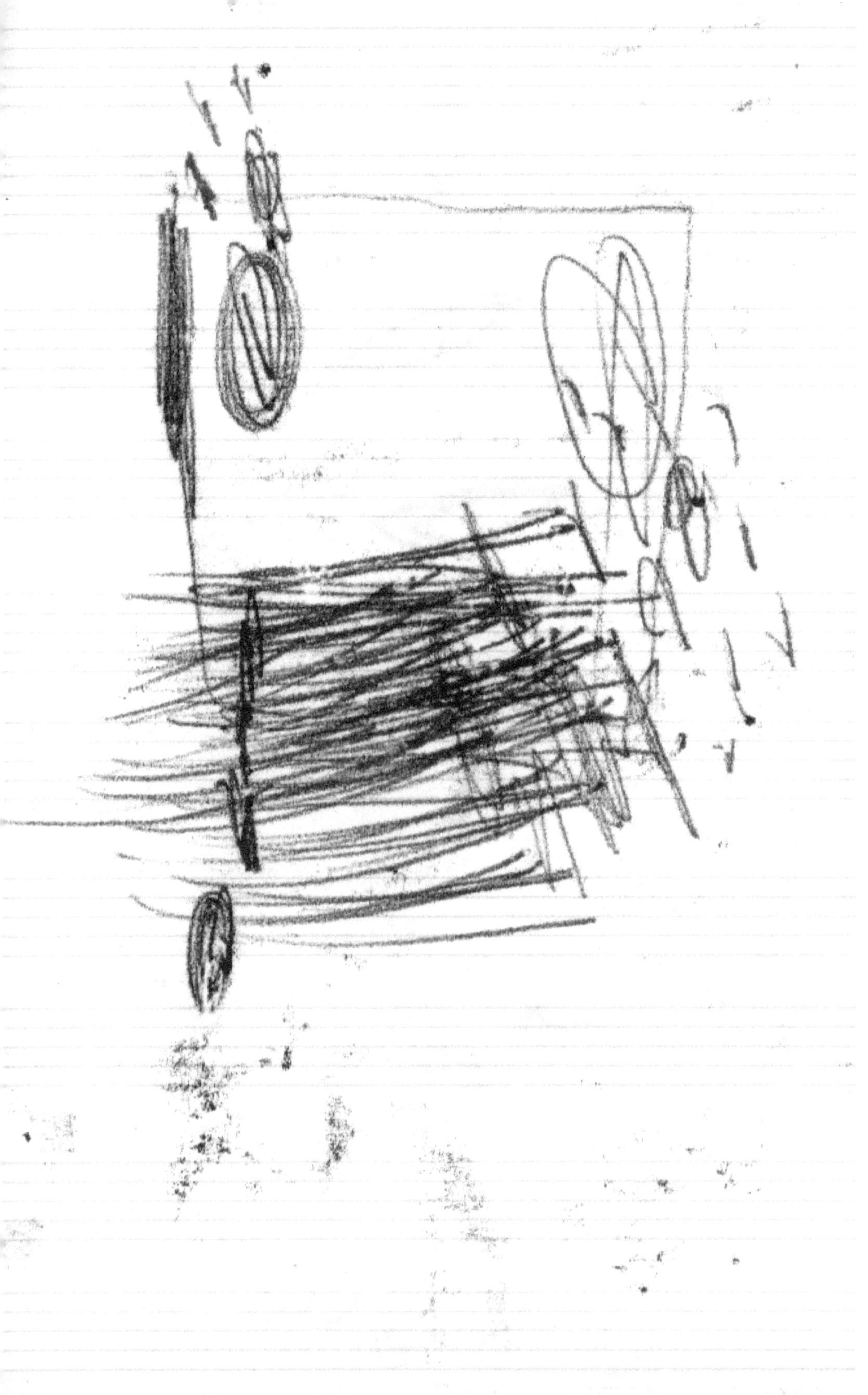

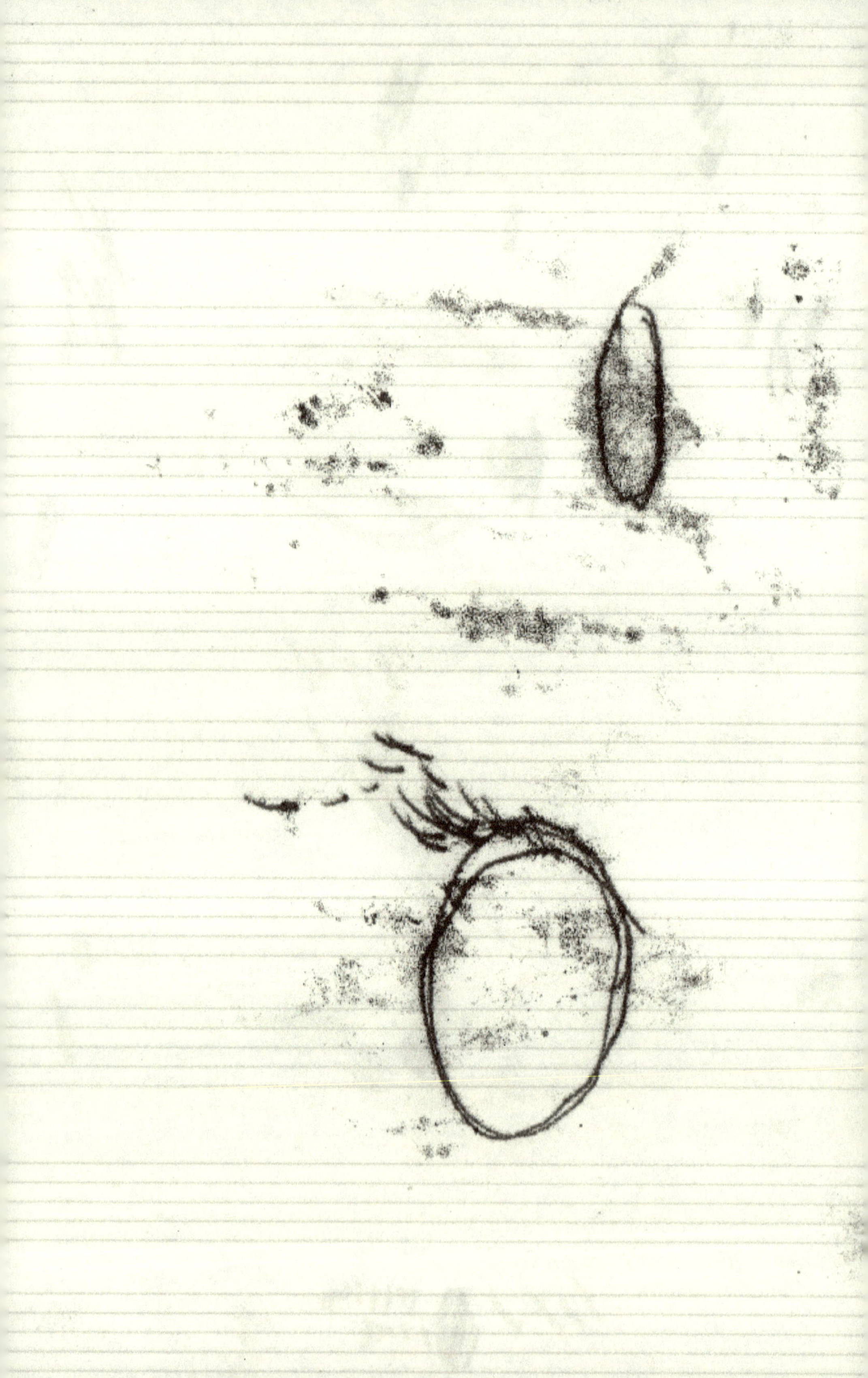

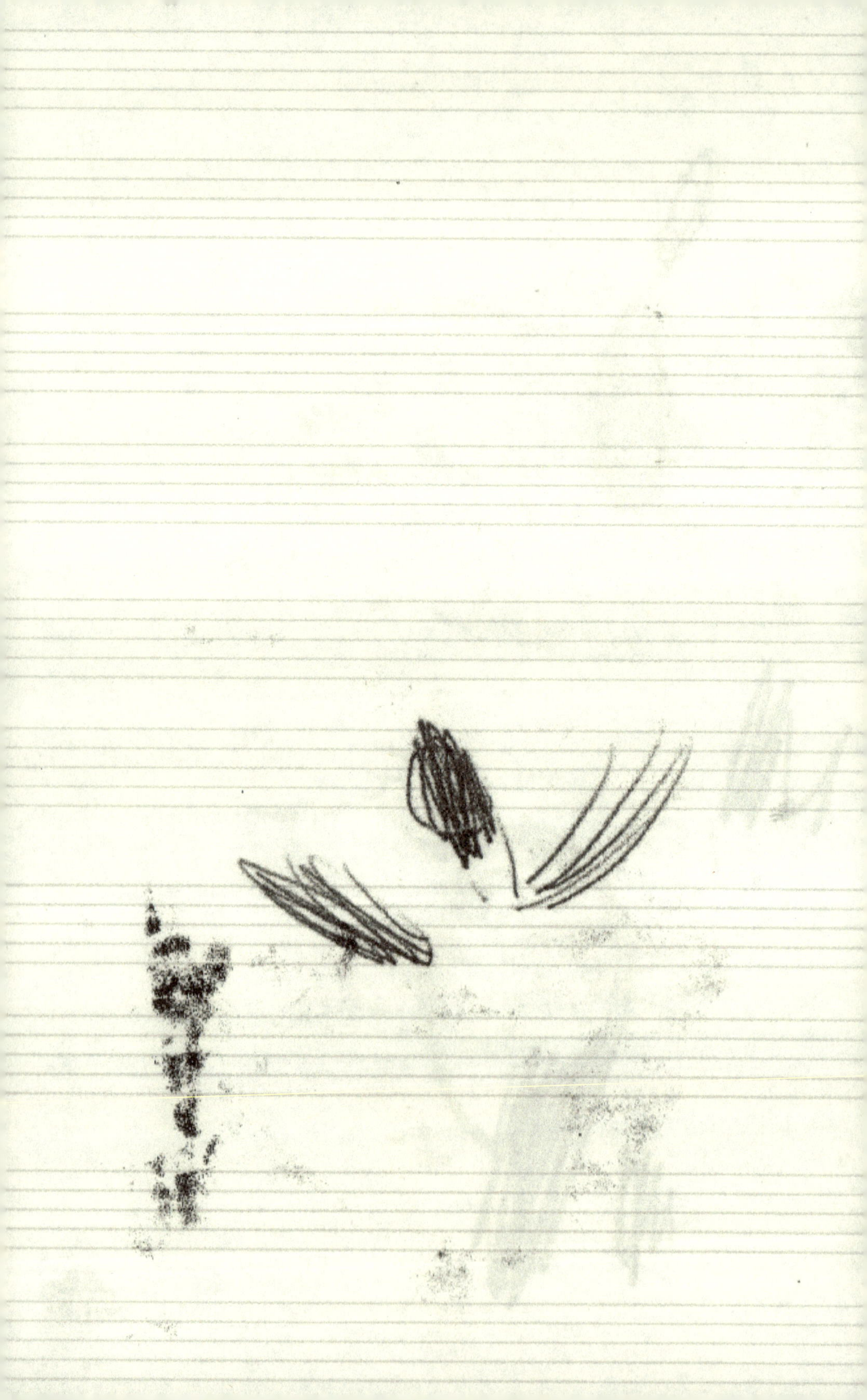

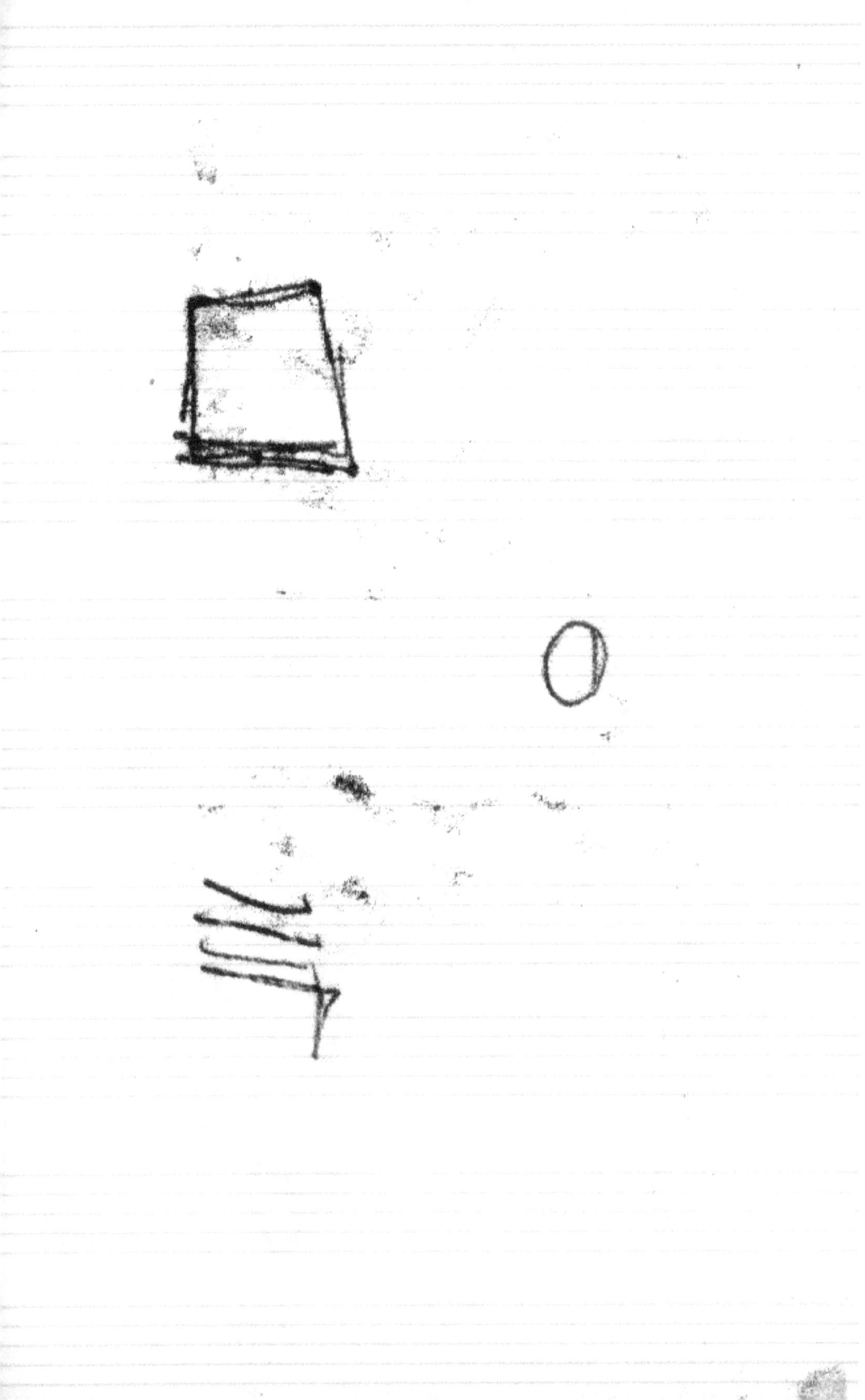

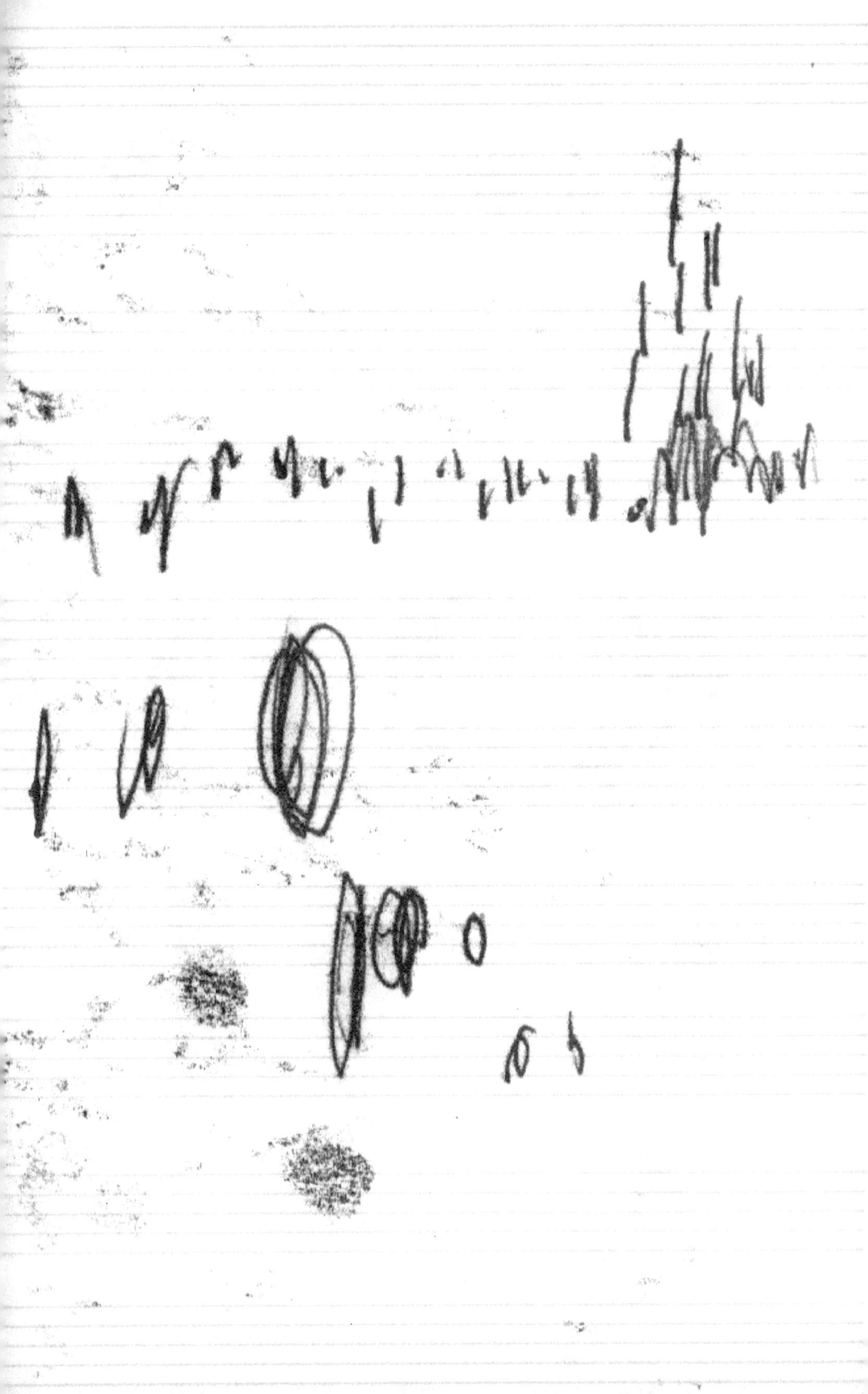

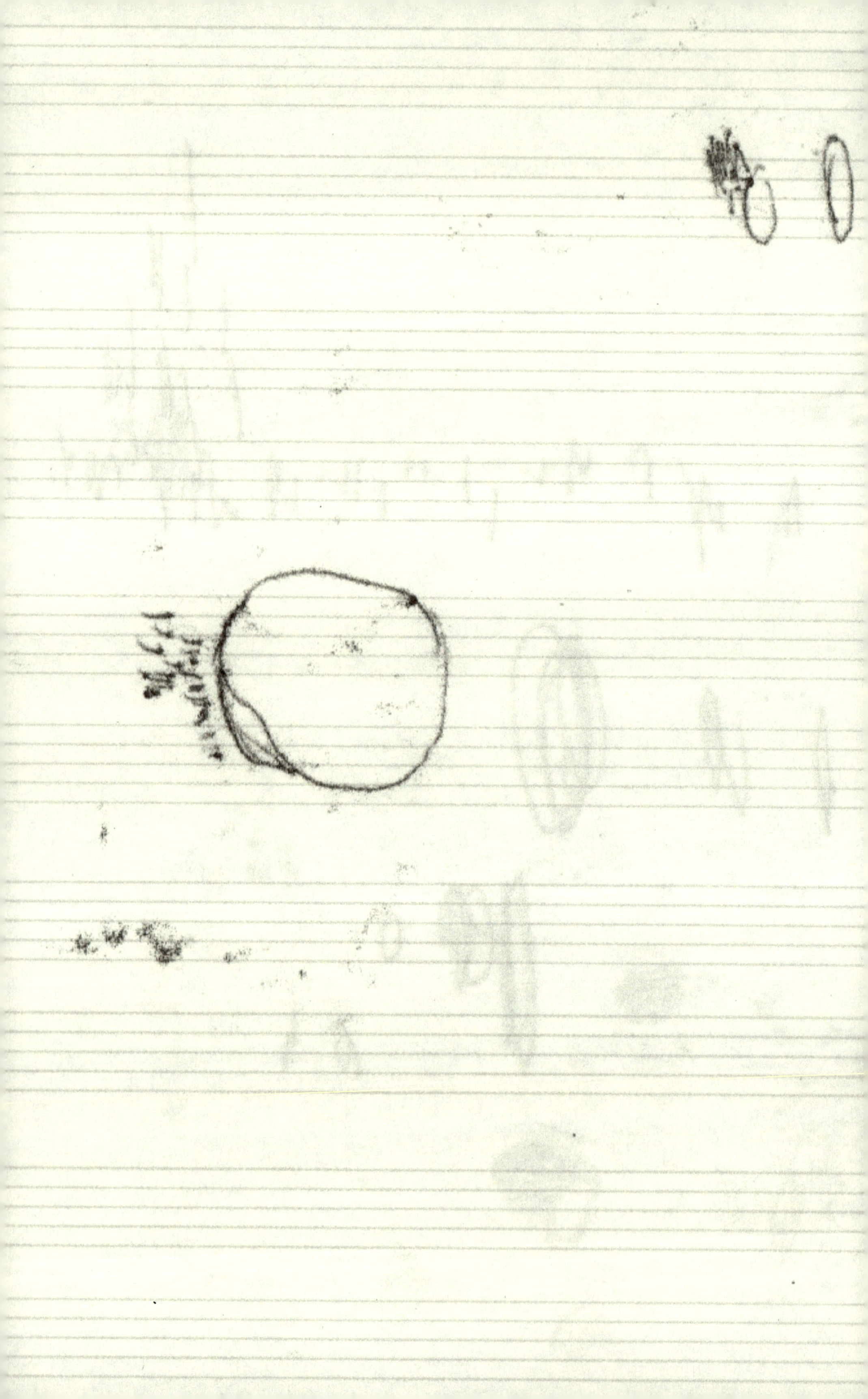

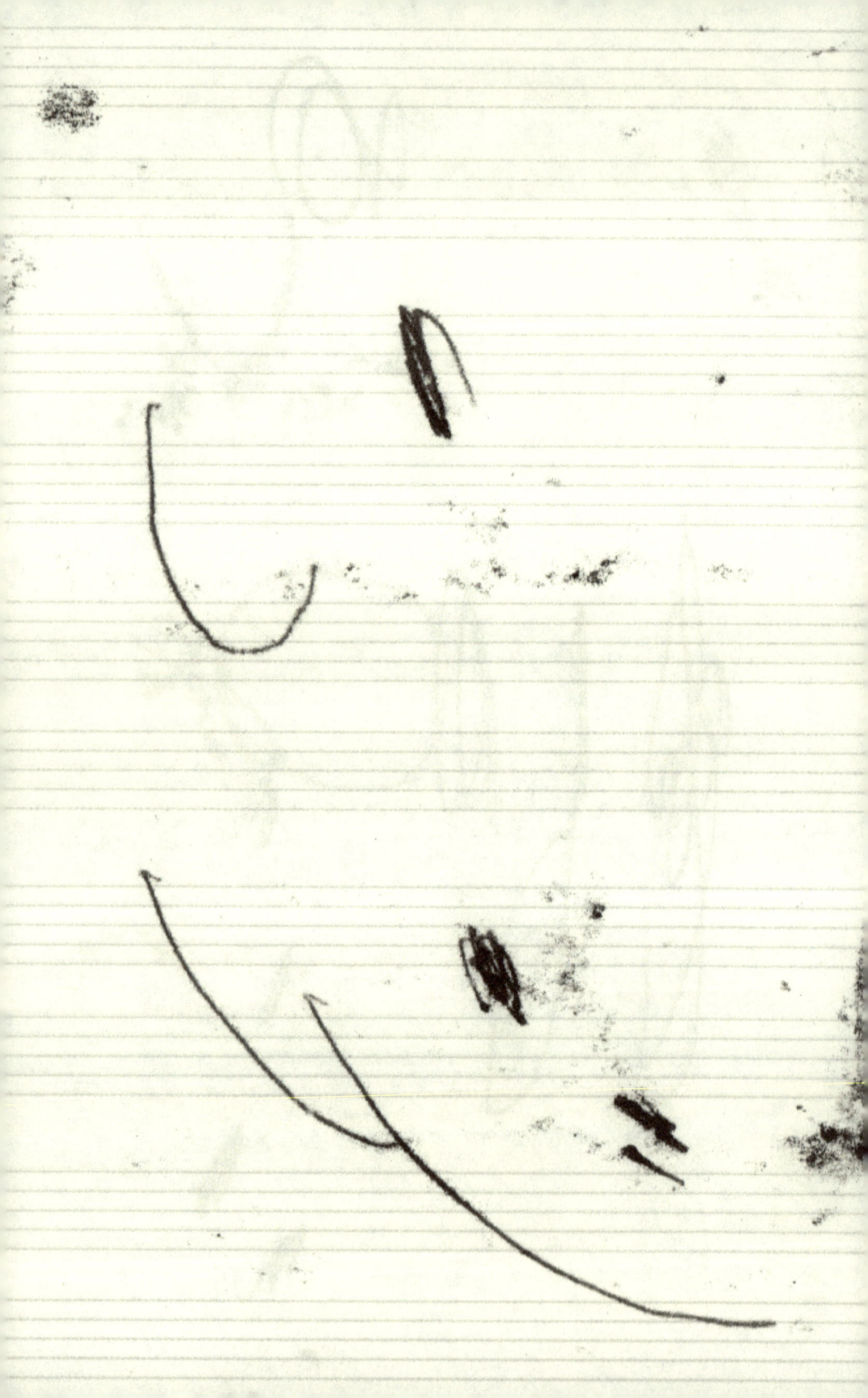

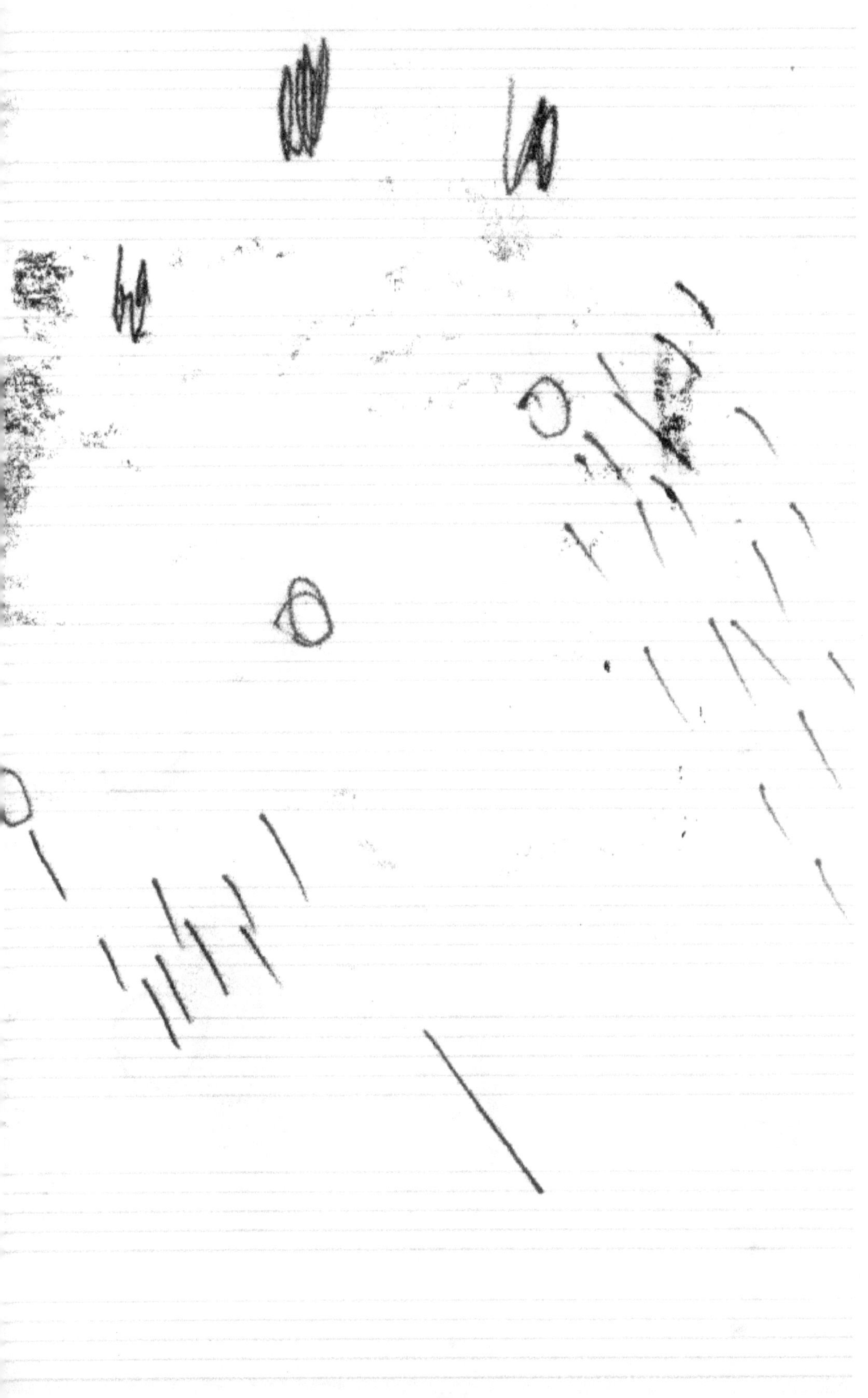

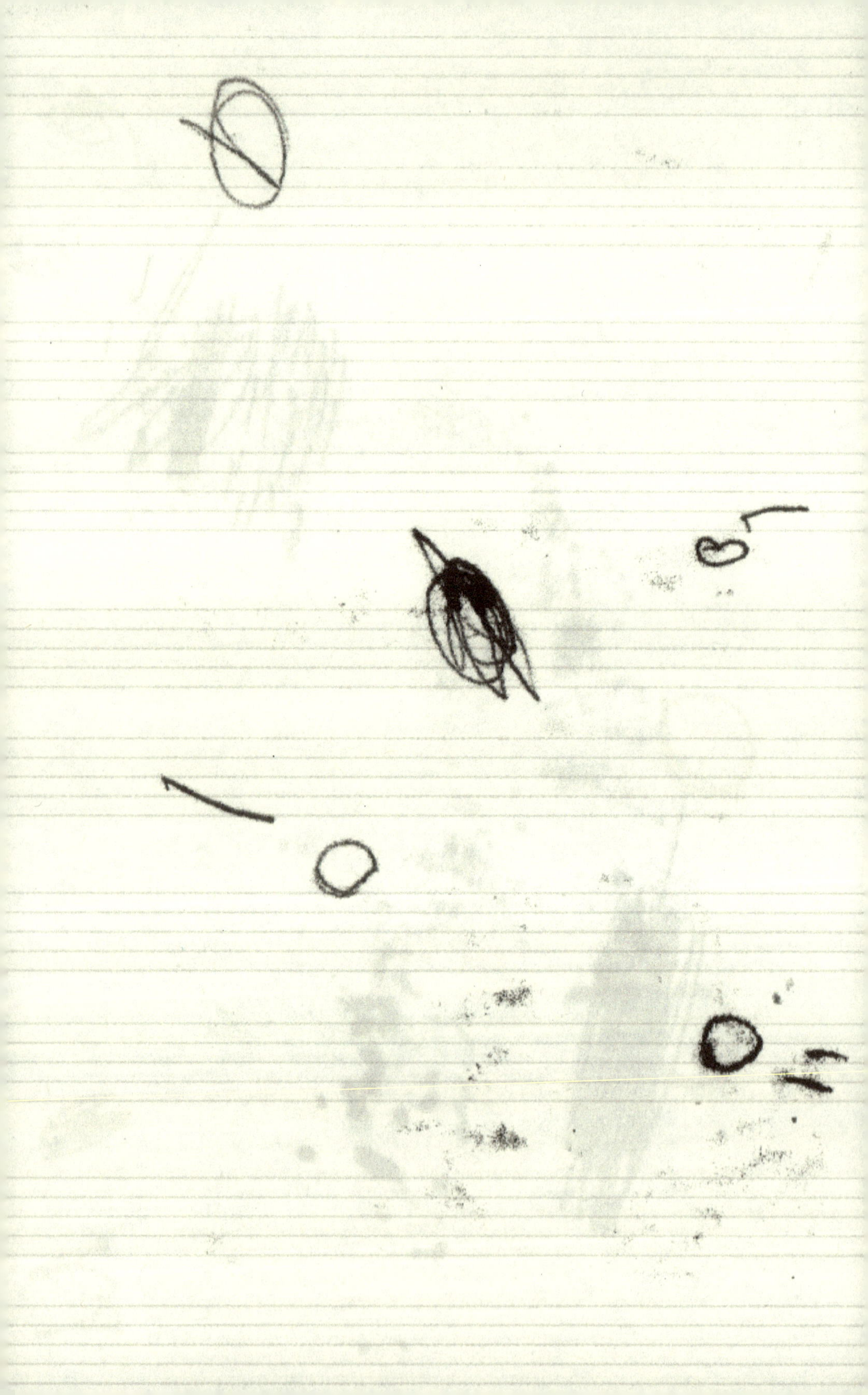

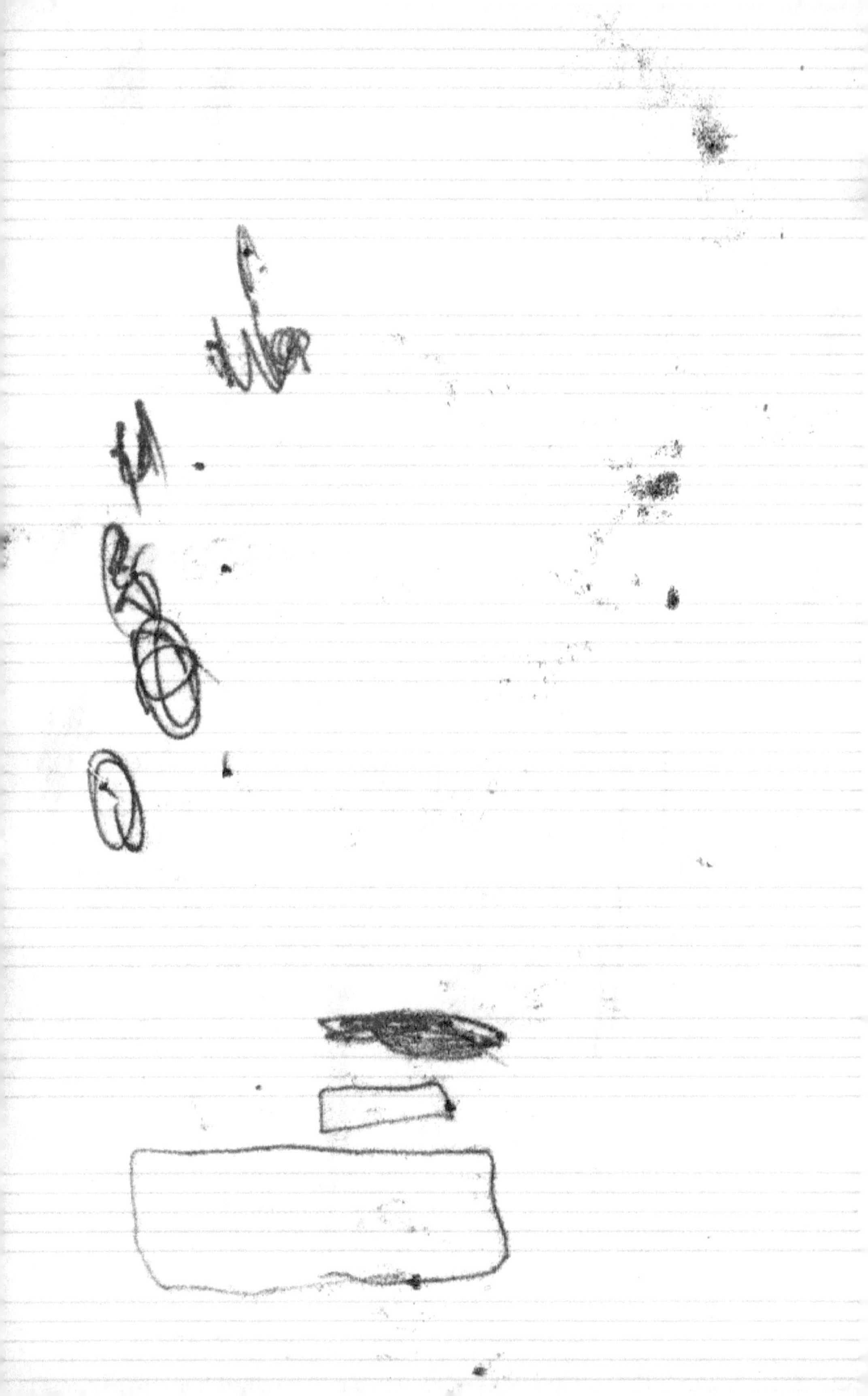

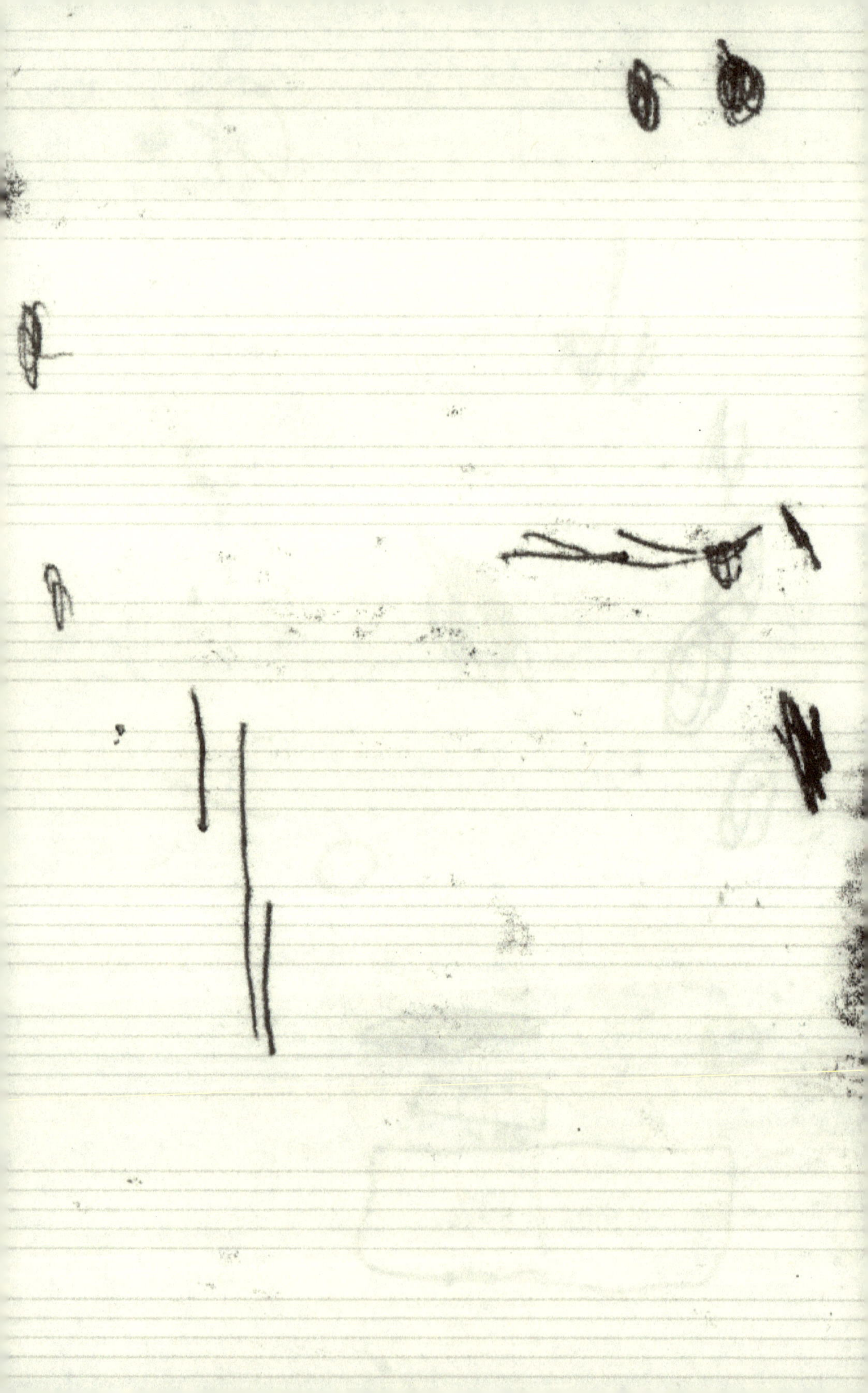

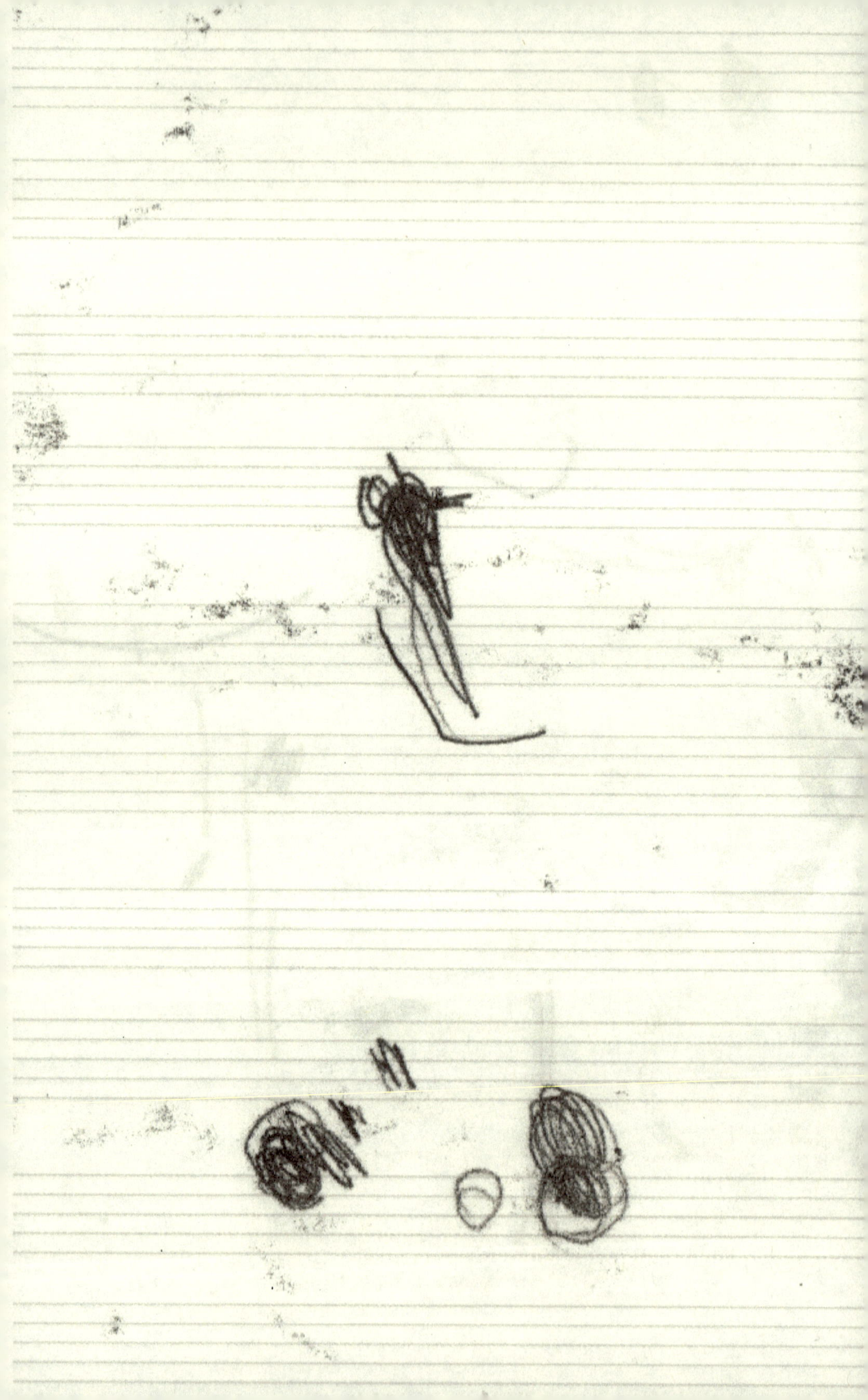

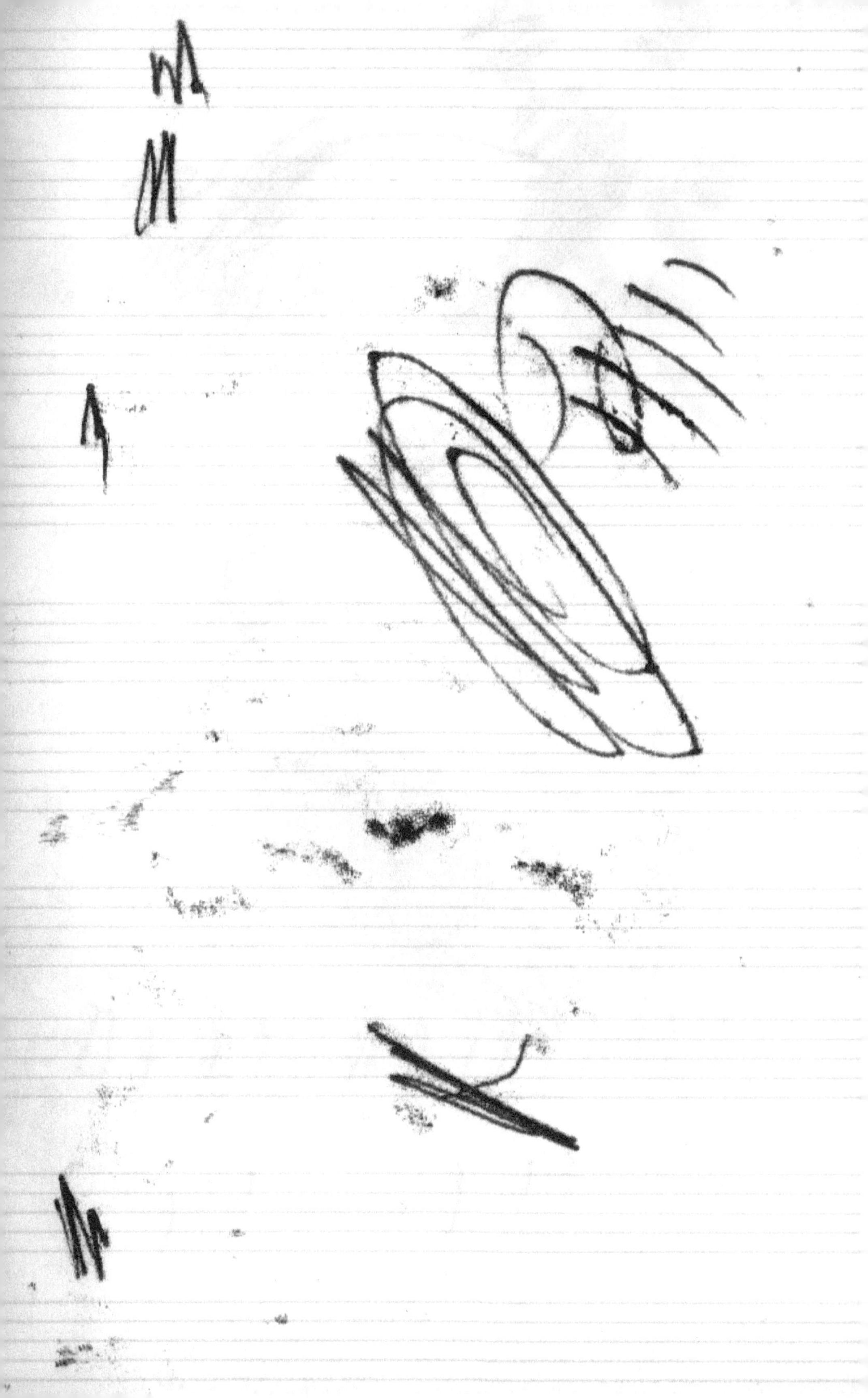

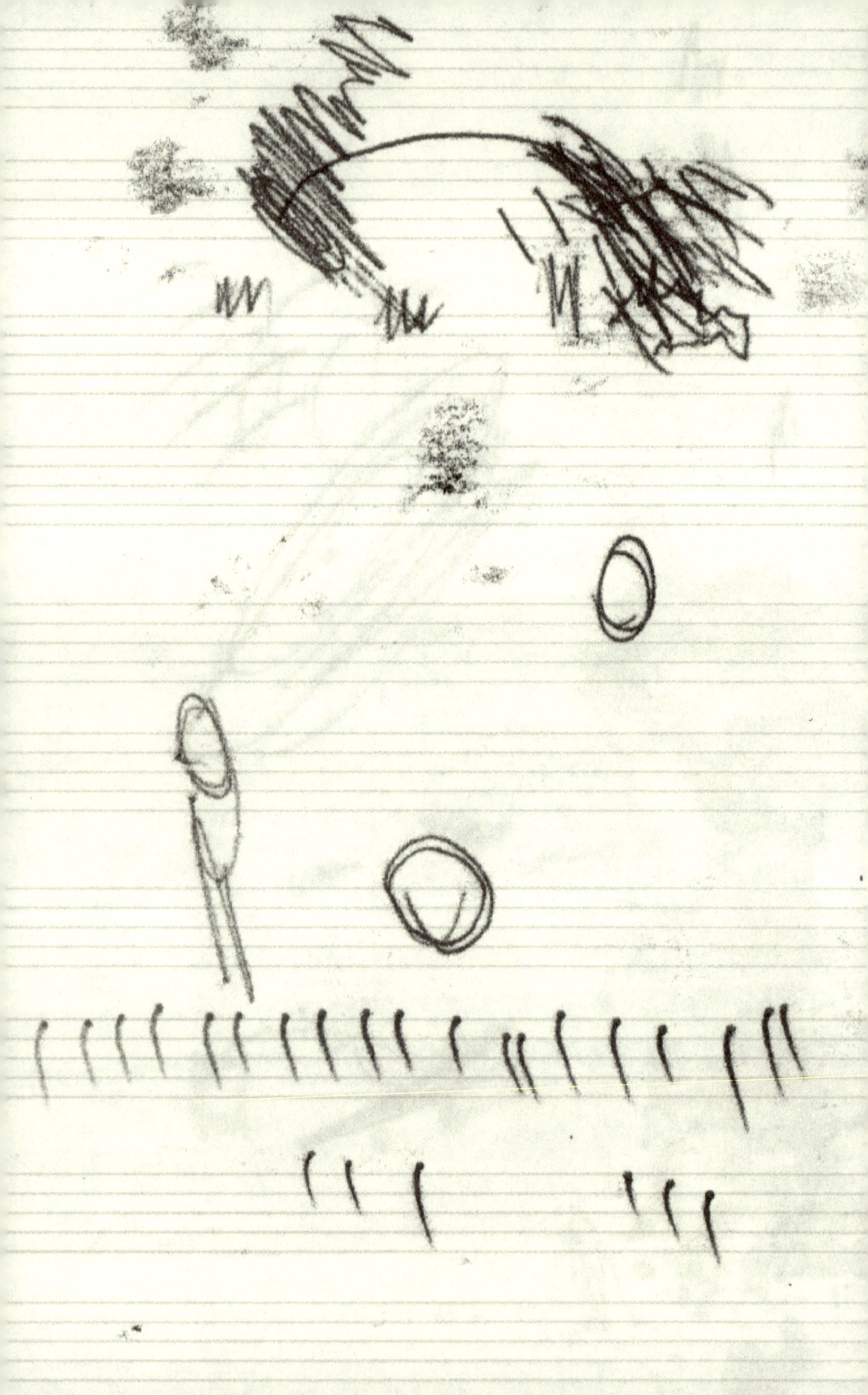

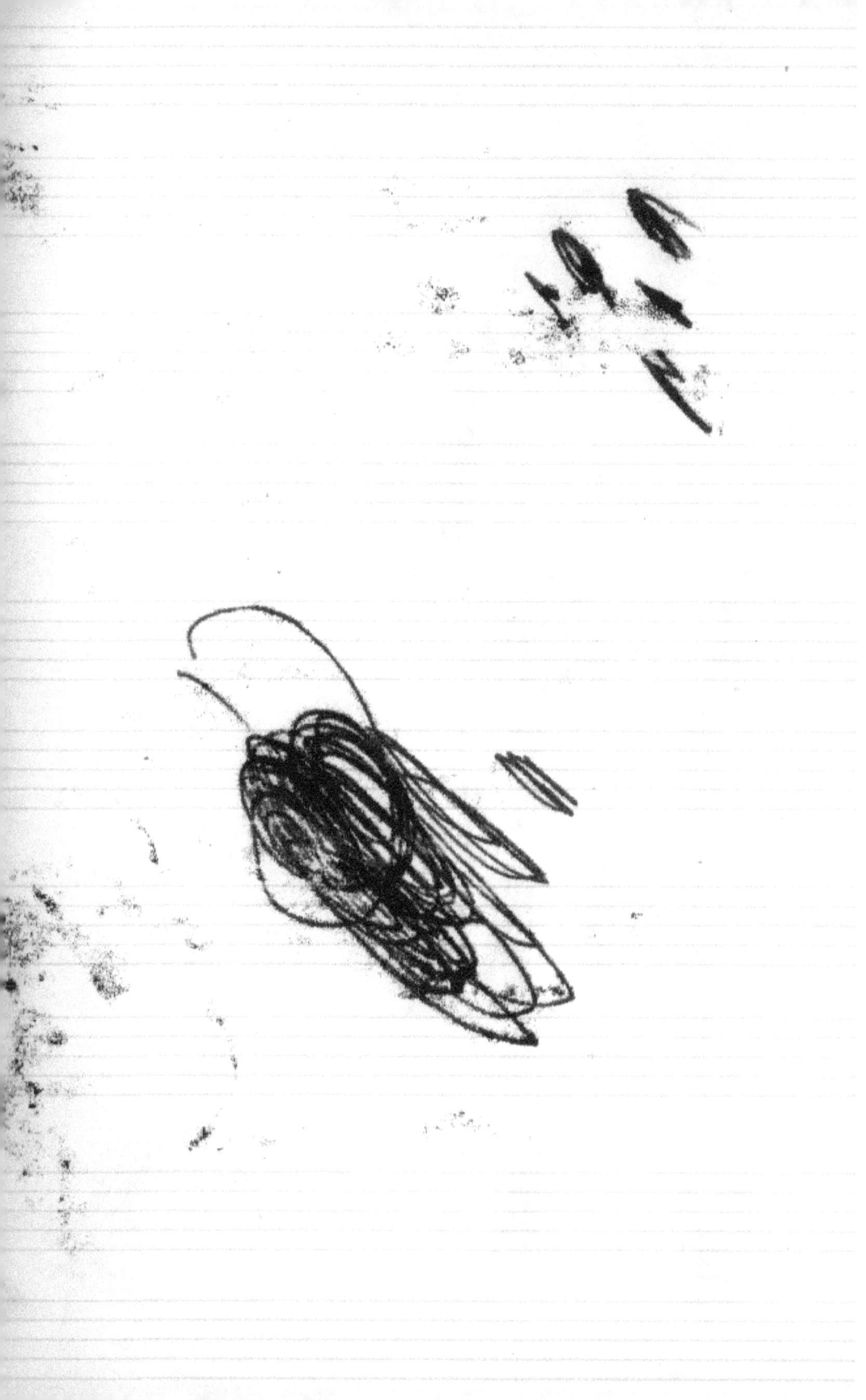

www.ingramcontent.com/pod-product-compliance
Lightning Source LLC
LaVergne TN
LVHW051020080826
845145LV00009B/2720

* 9 7 8 1 7 3 4 7 5 4 5 6 8 *